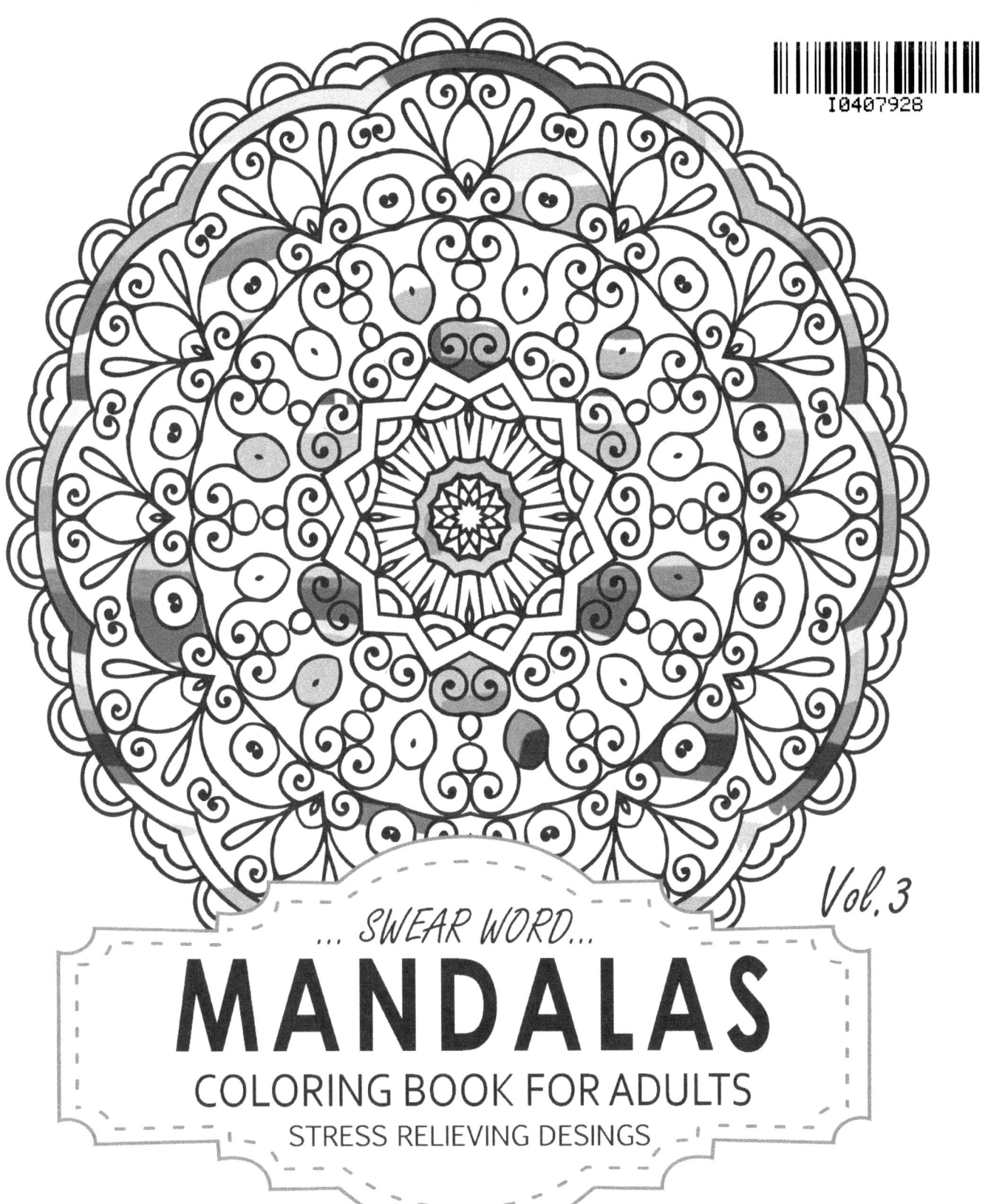

Vol.3

...*SWEAR WORD*...

MANDALAS

COLORING BOOK FOR ADULTS

STRESS RELIEVING DESINGS

TEST YOUR COLOR

TEST YOUR COLOR

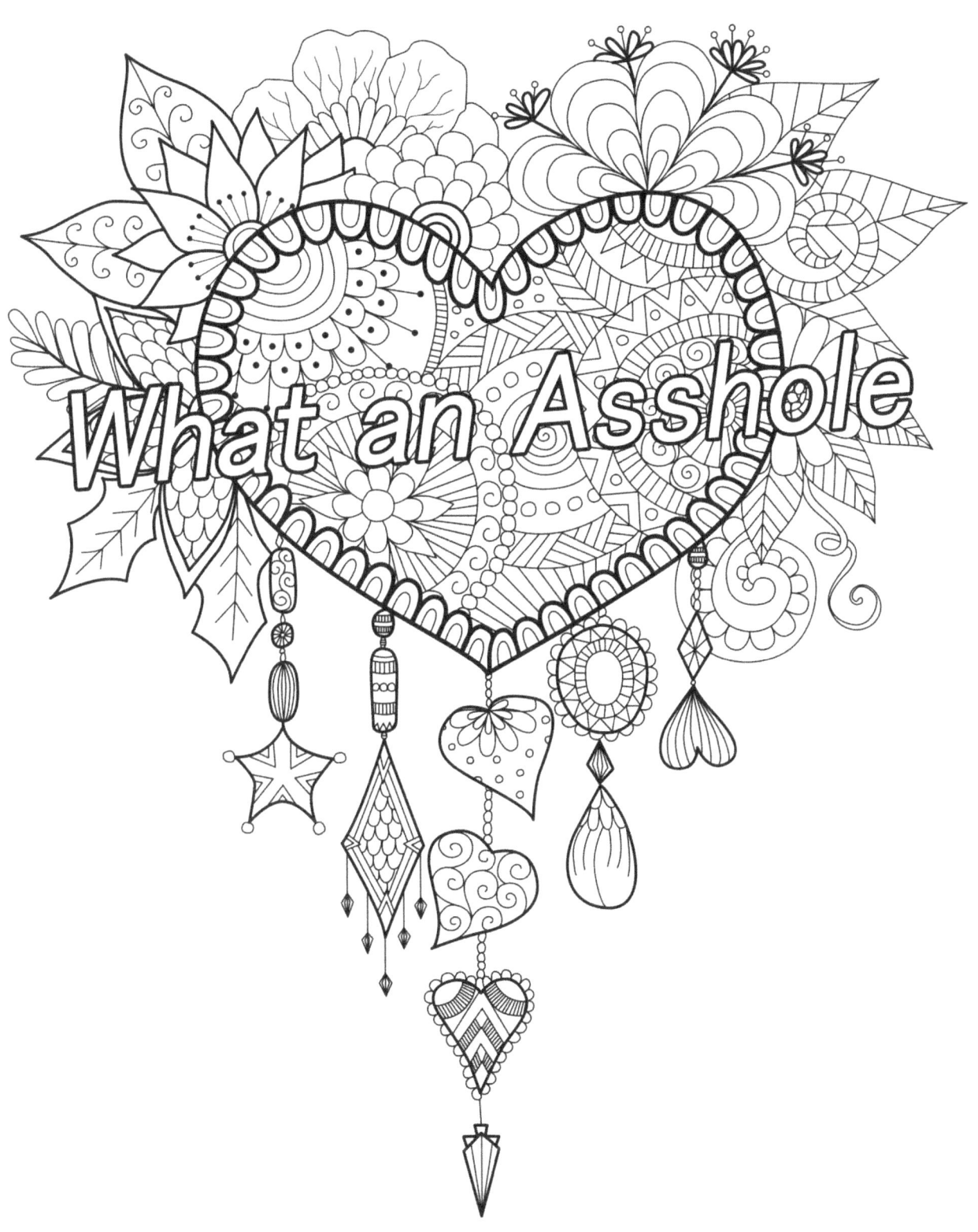

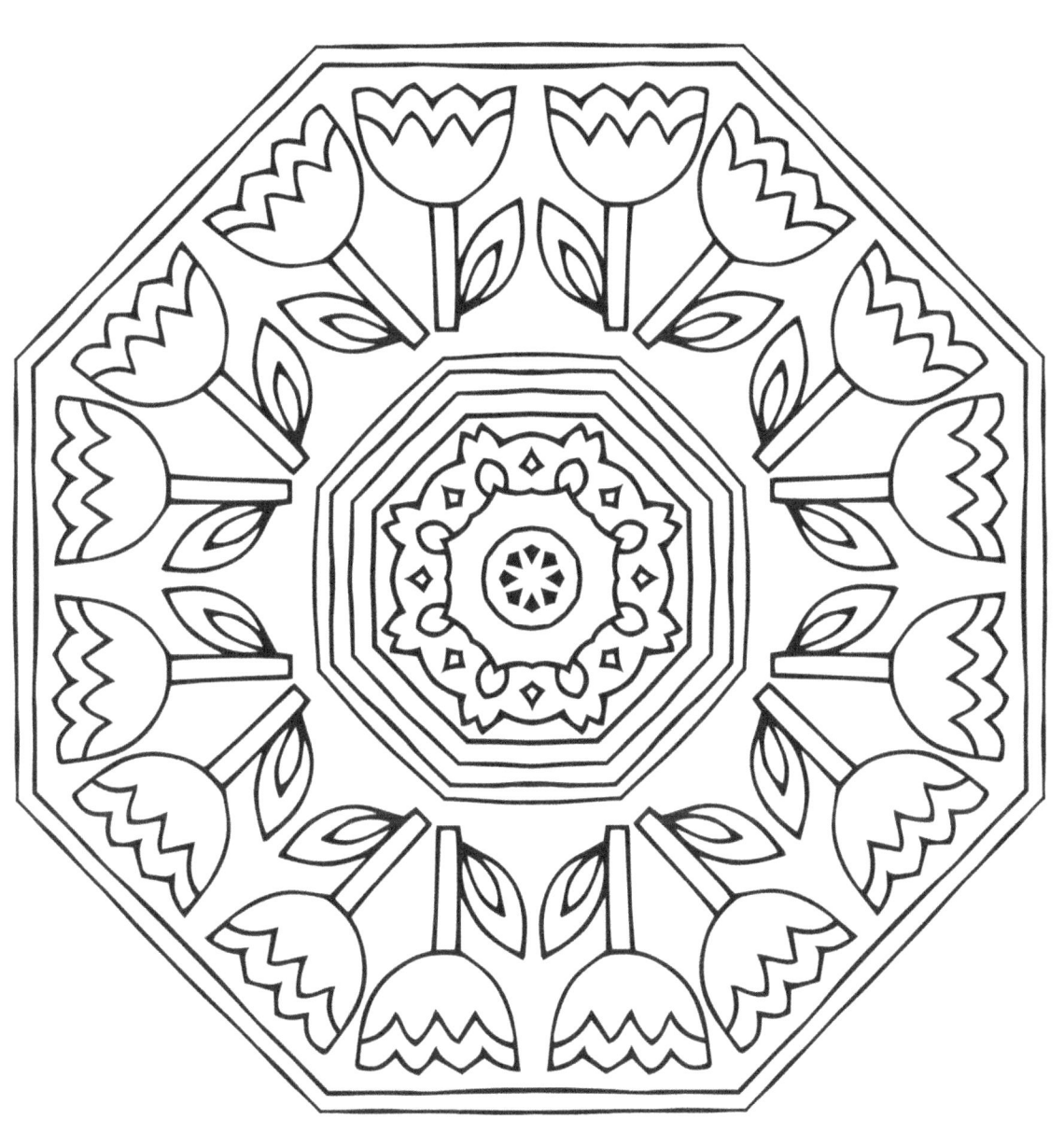

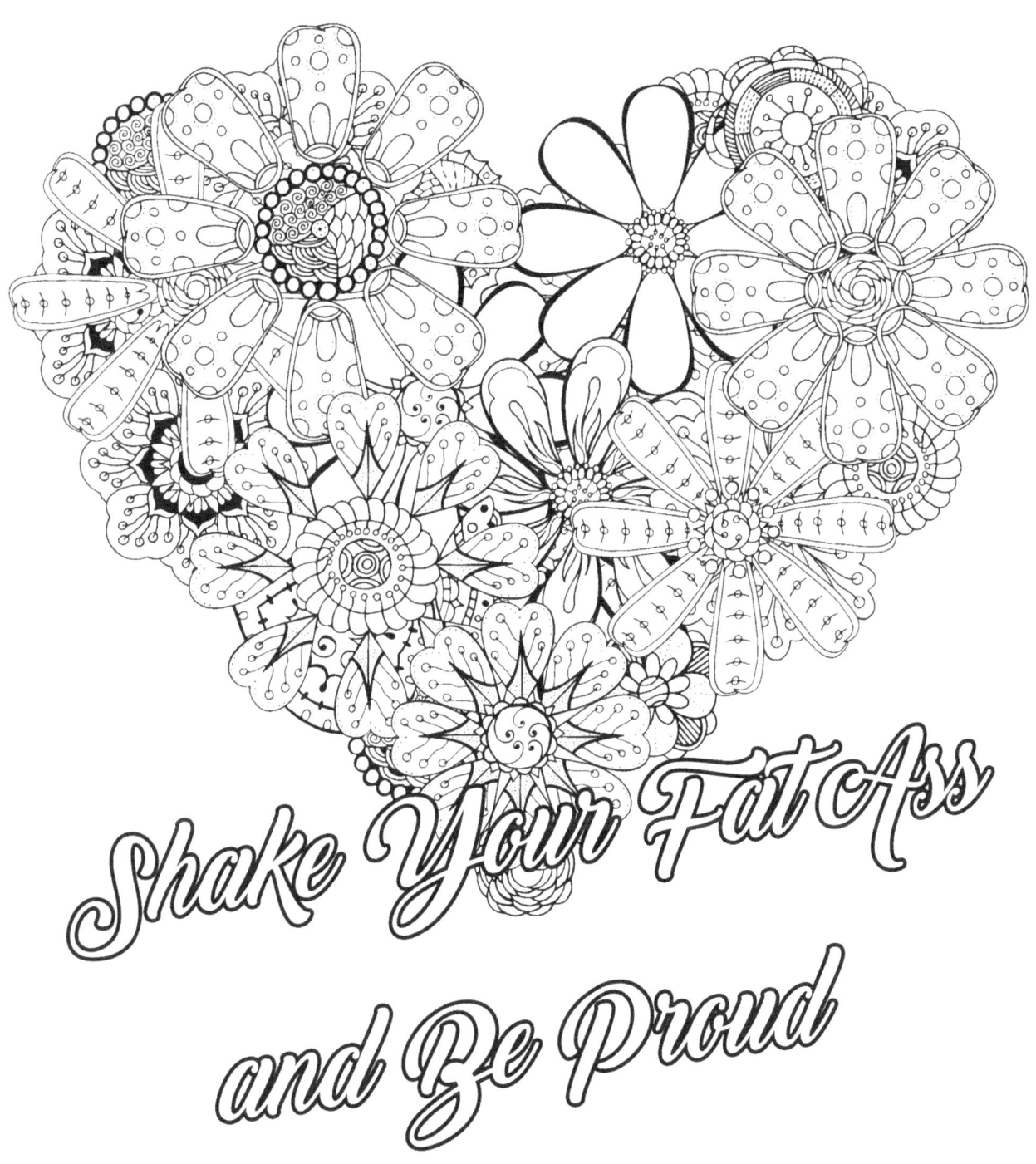

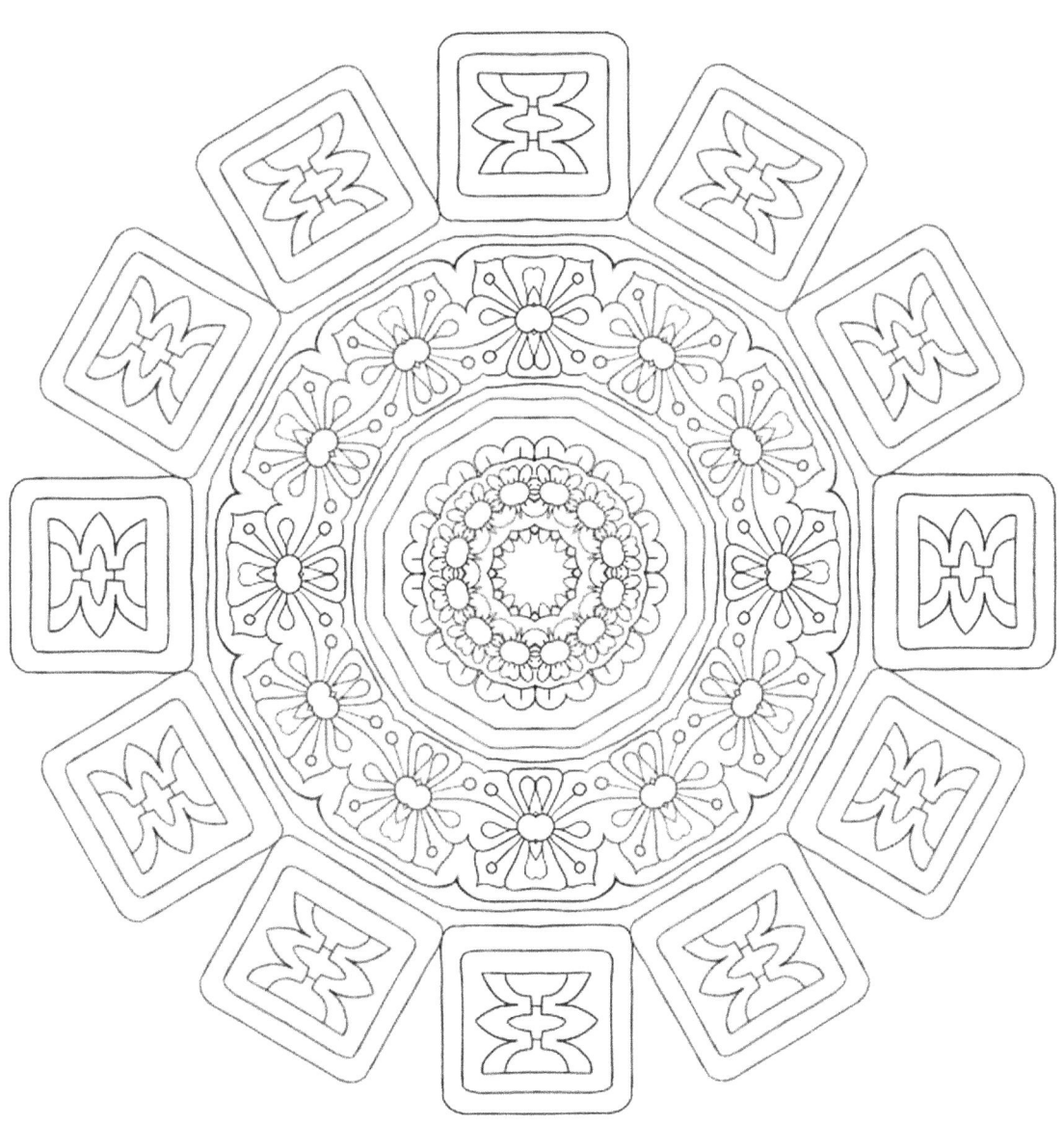

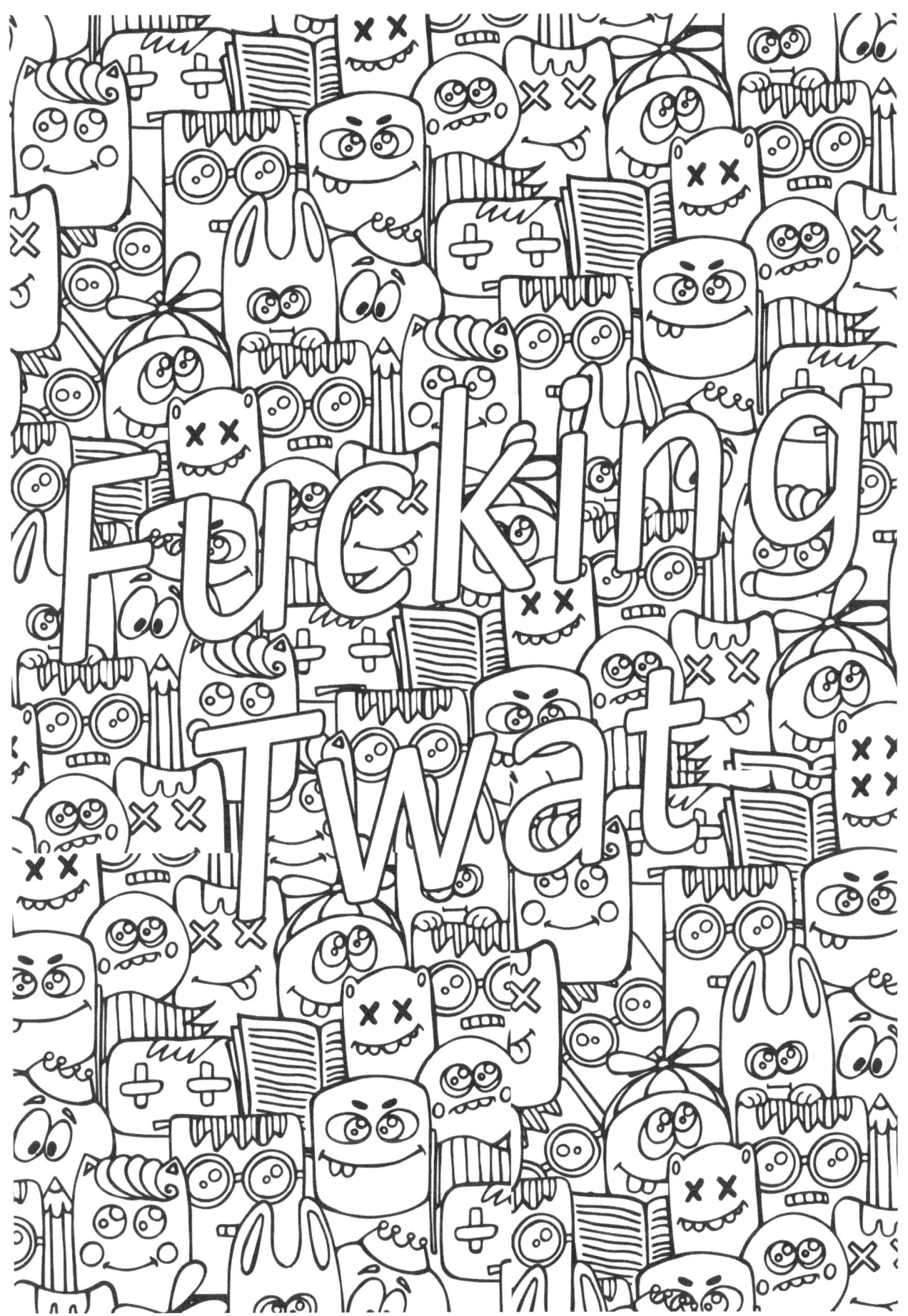

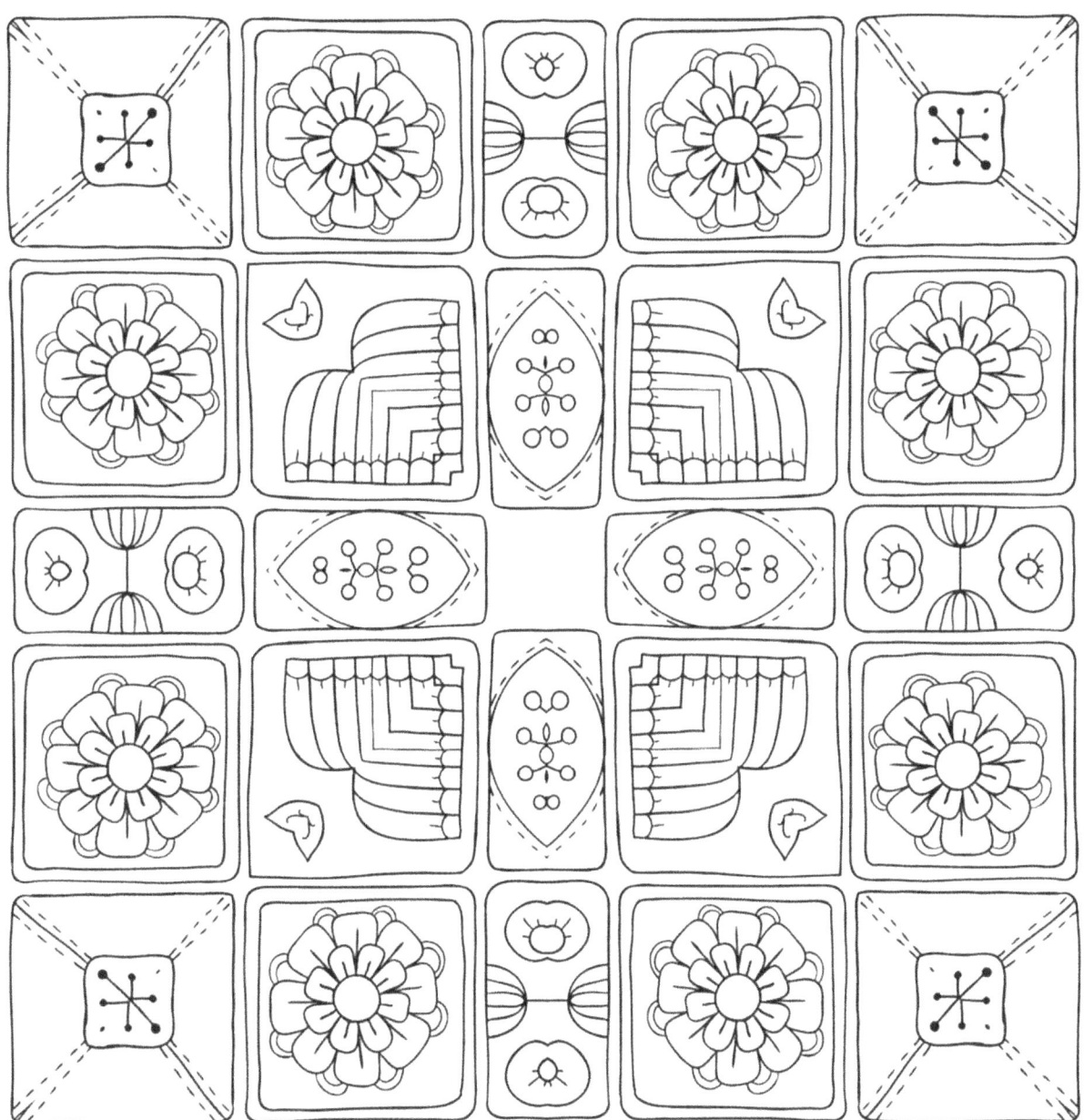

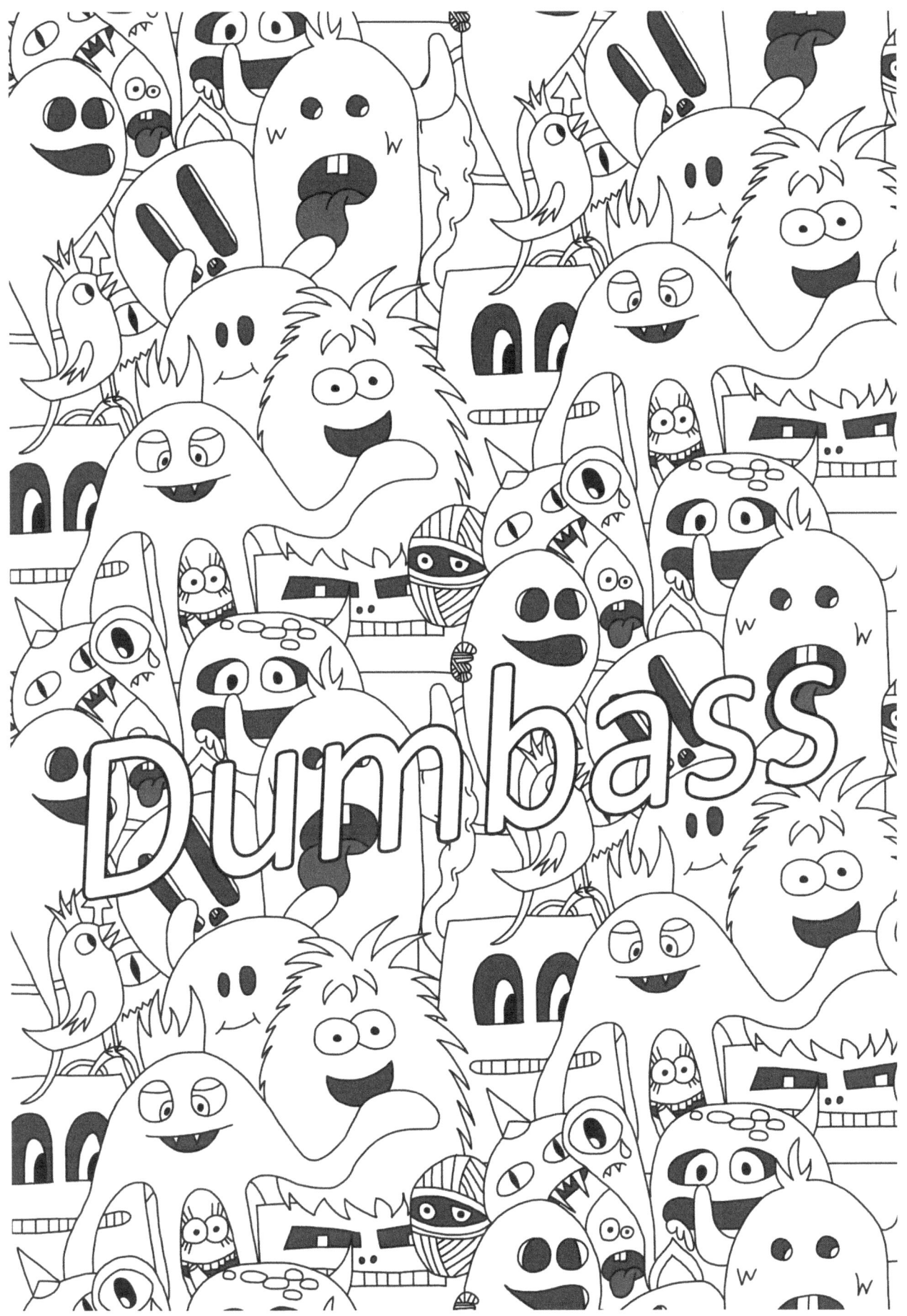

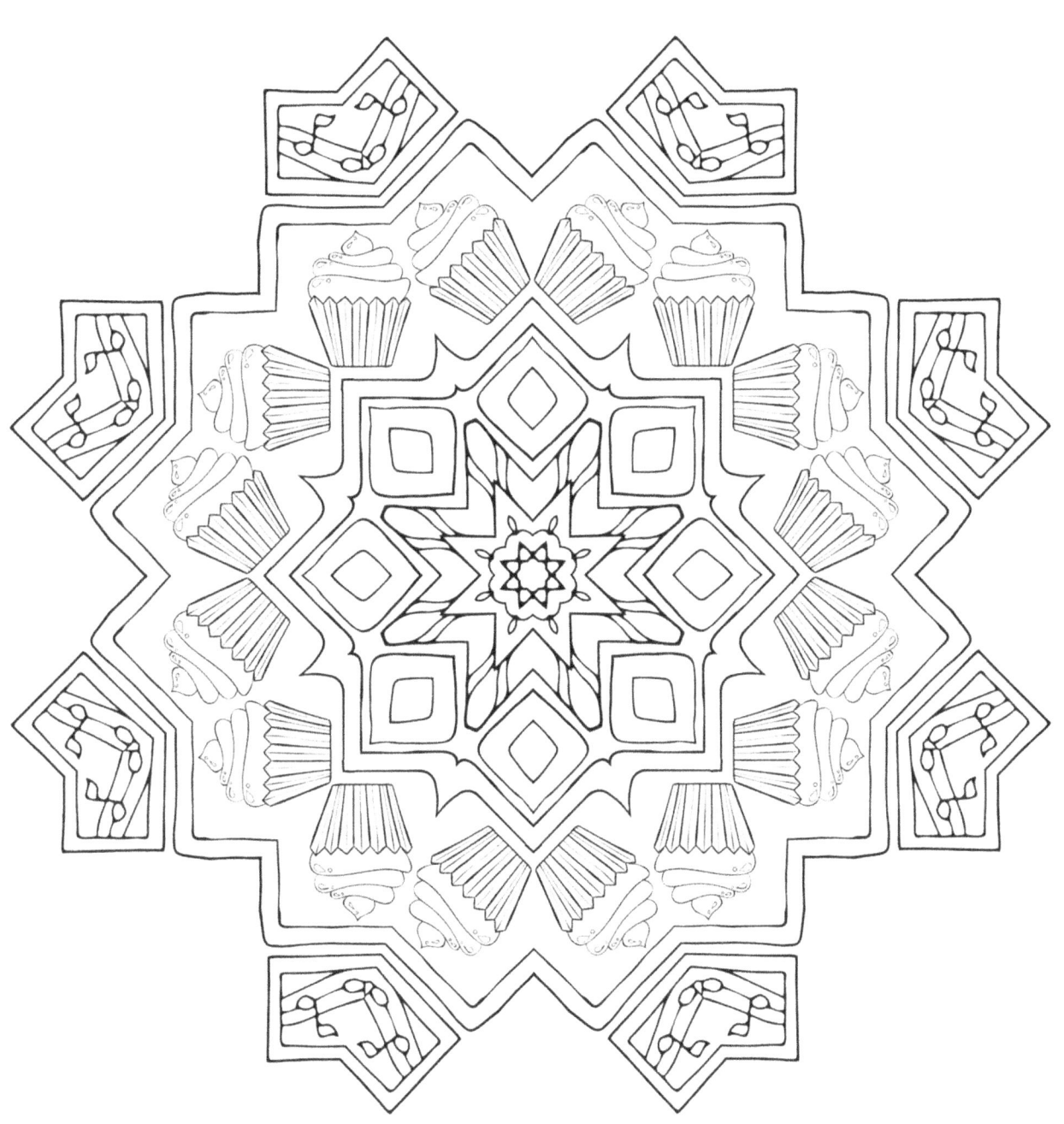

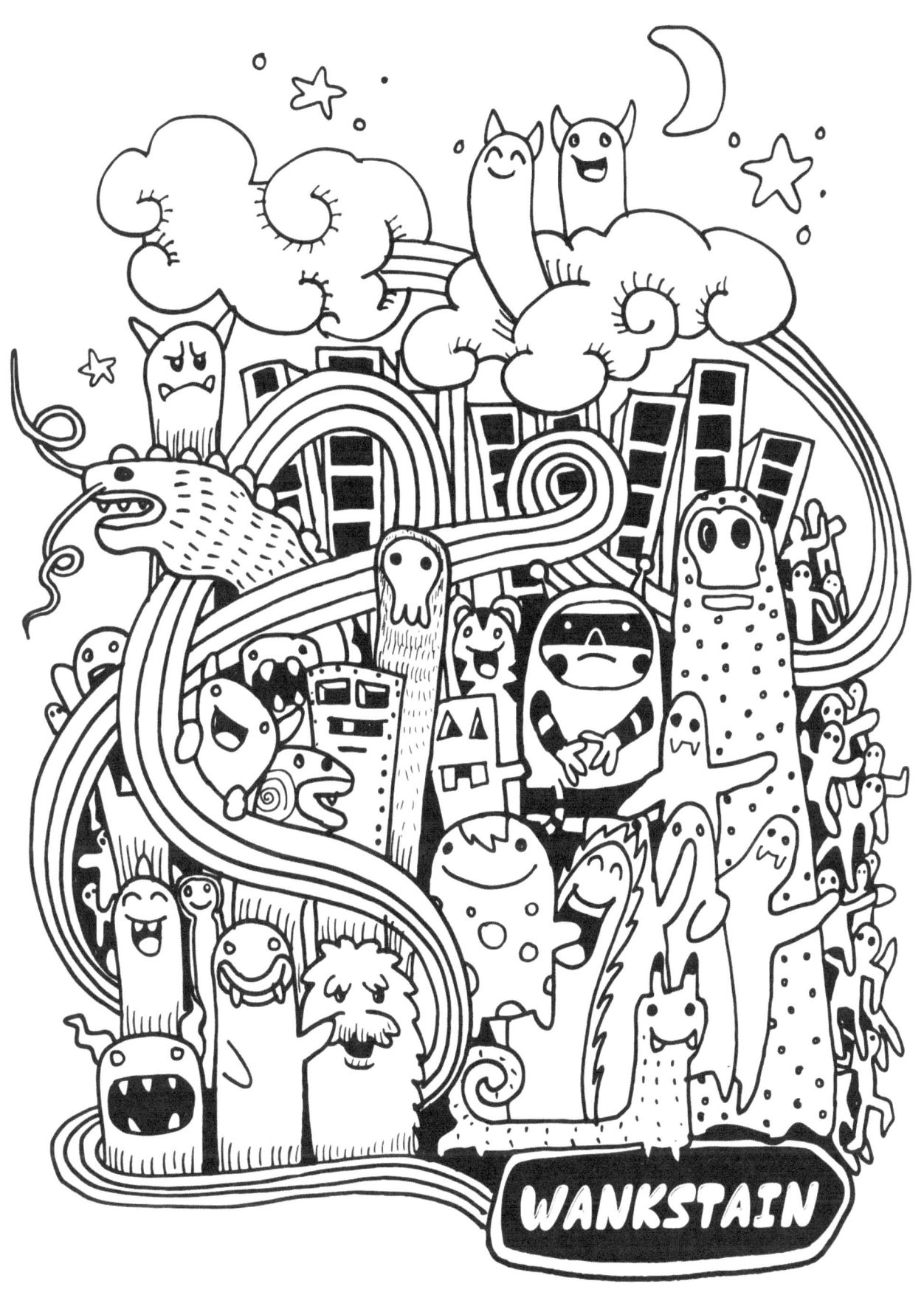

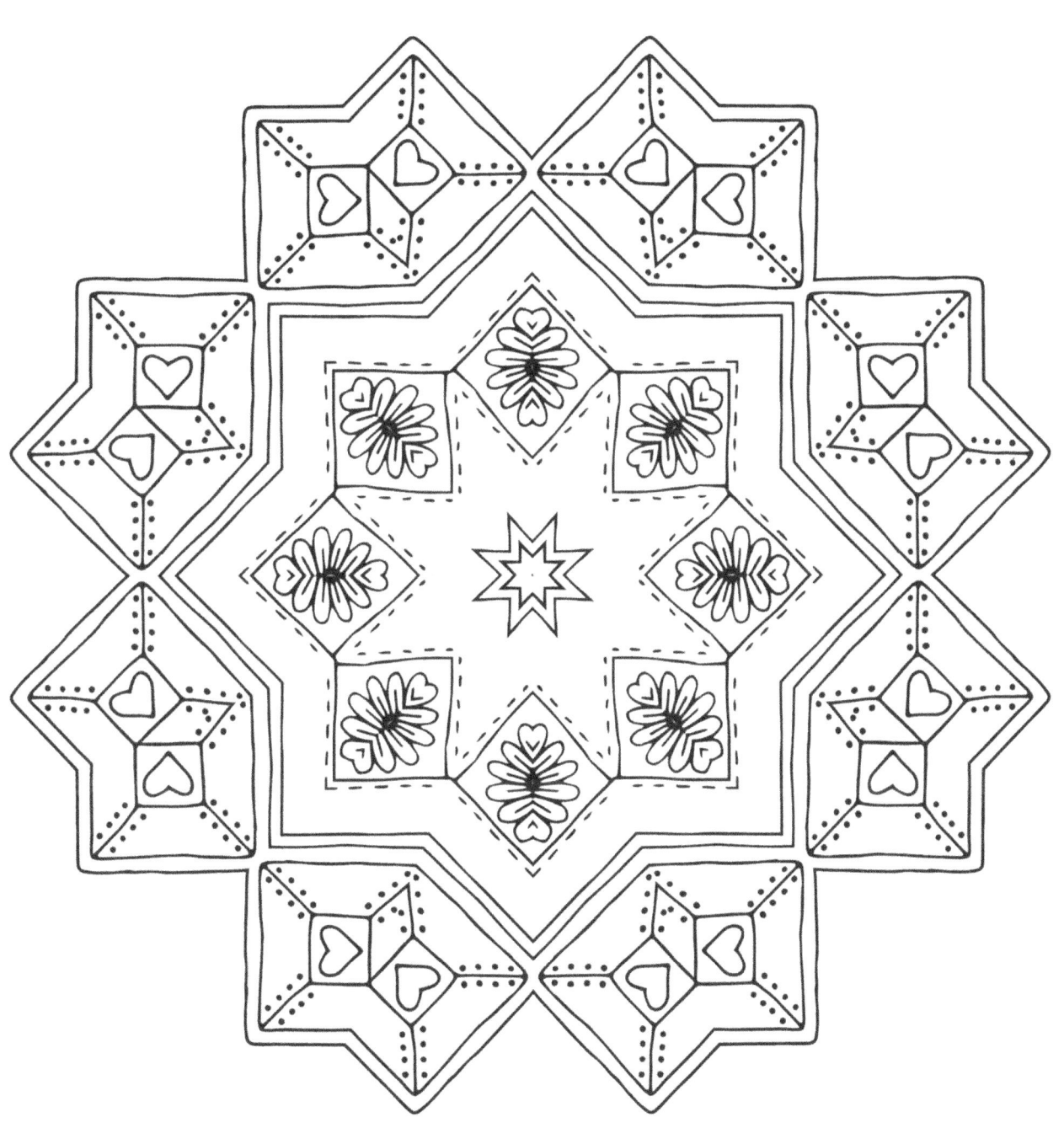

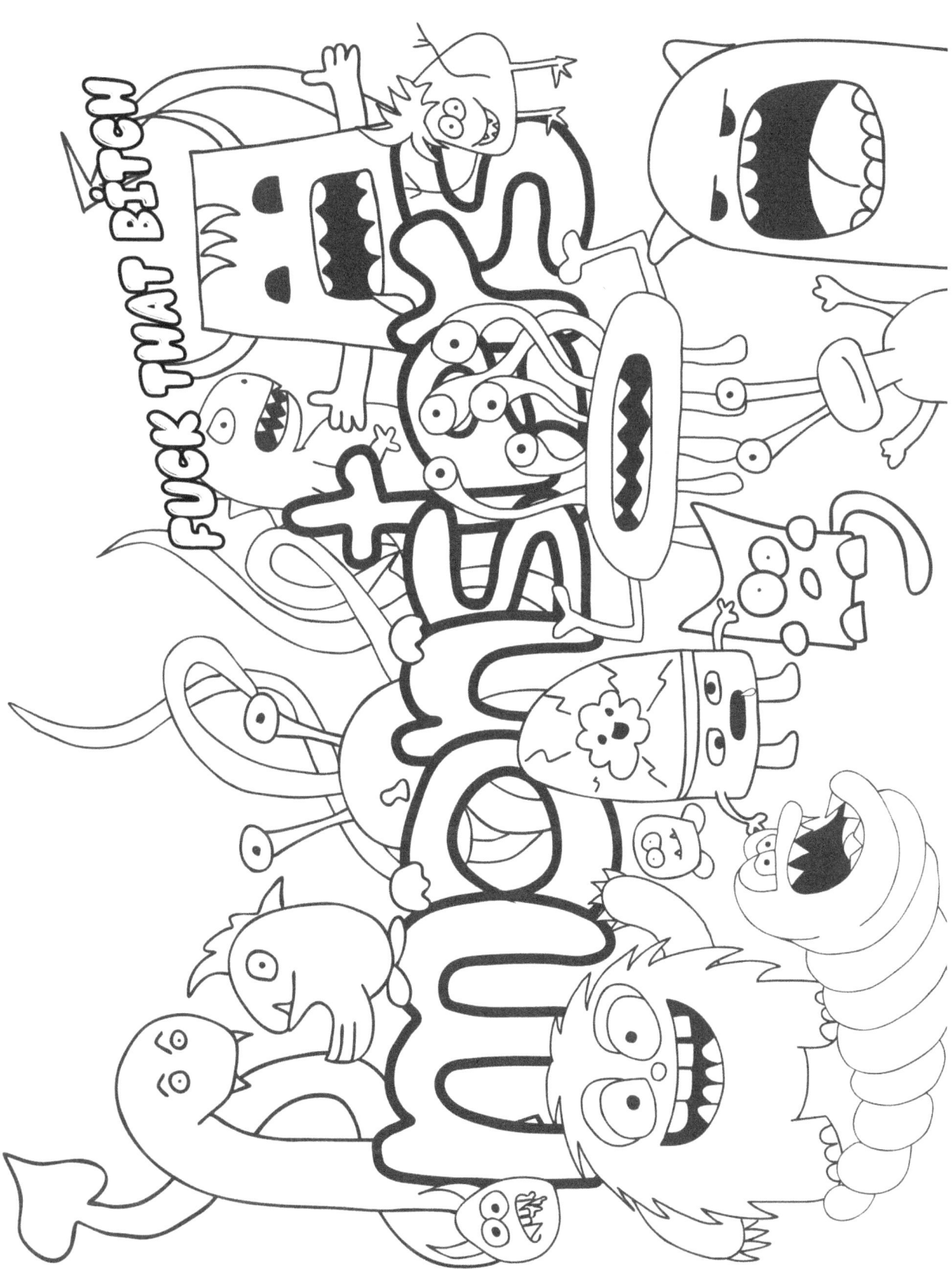

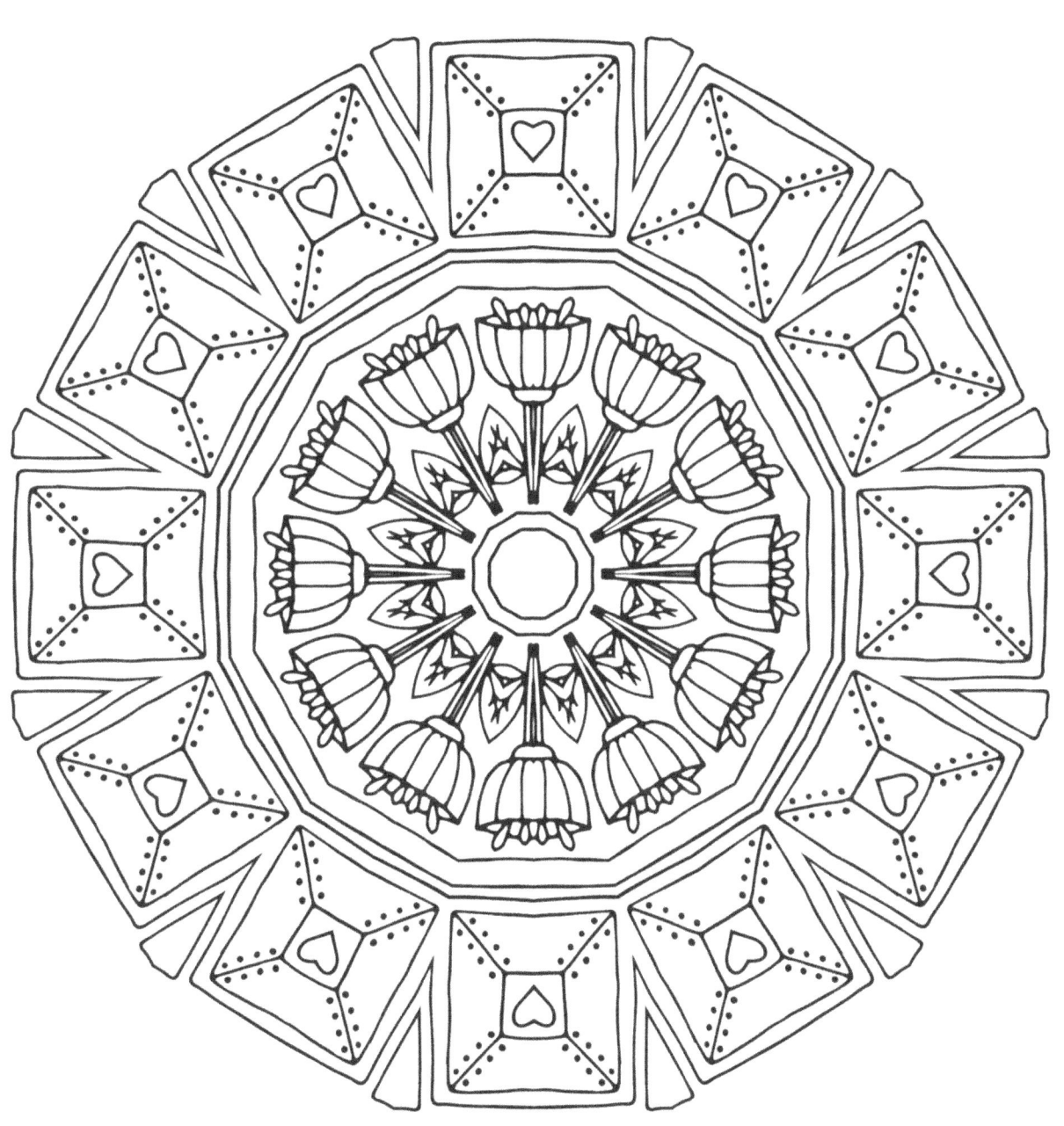

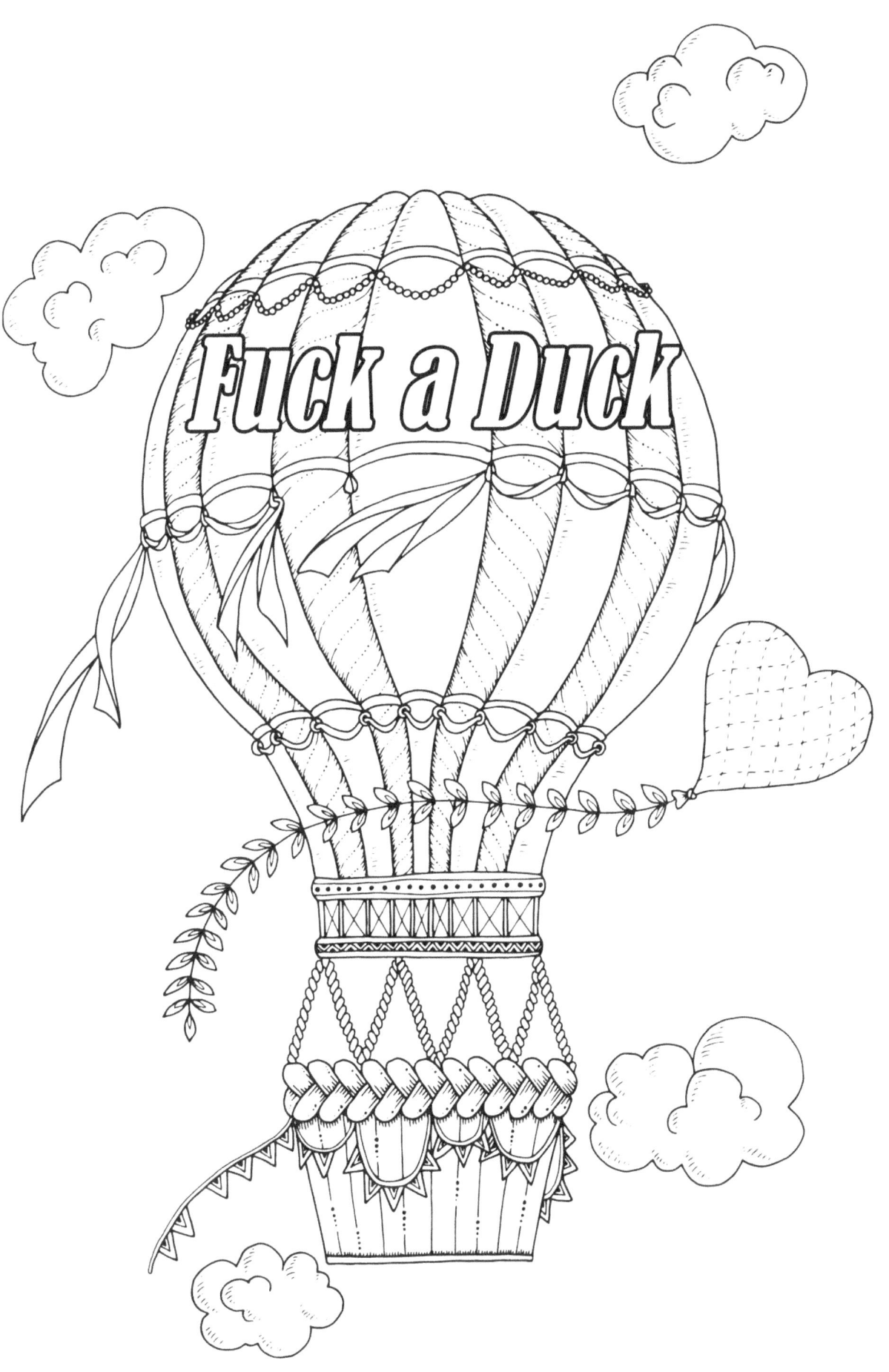

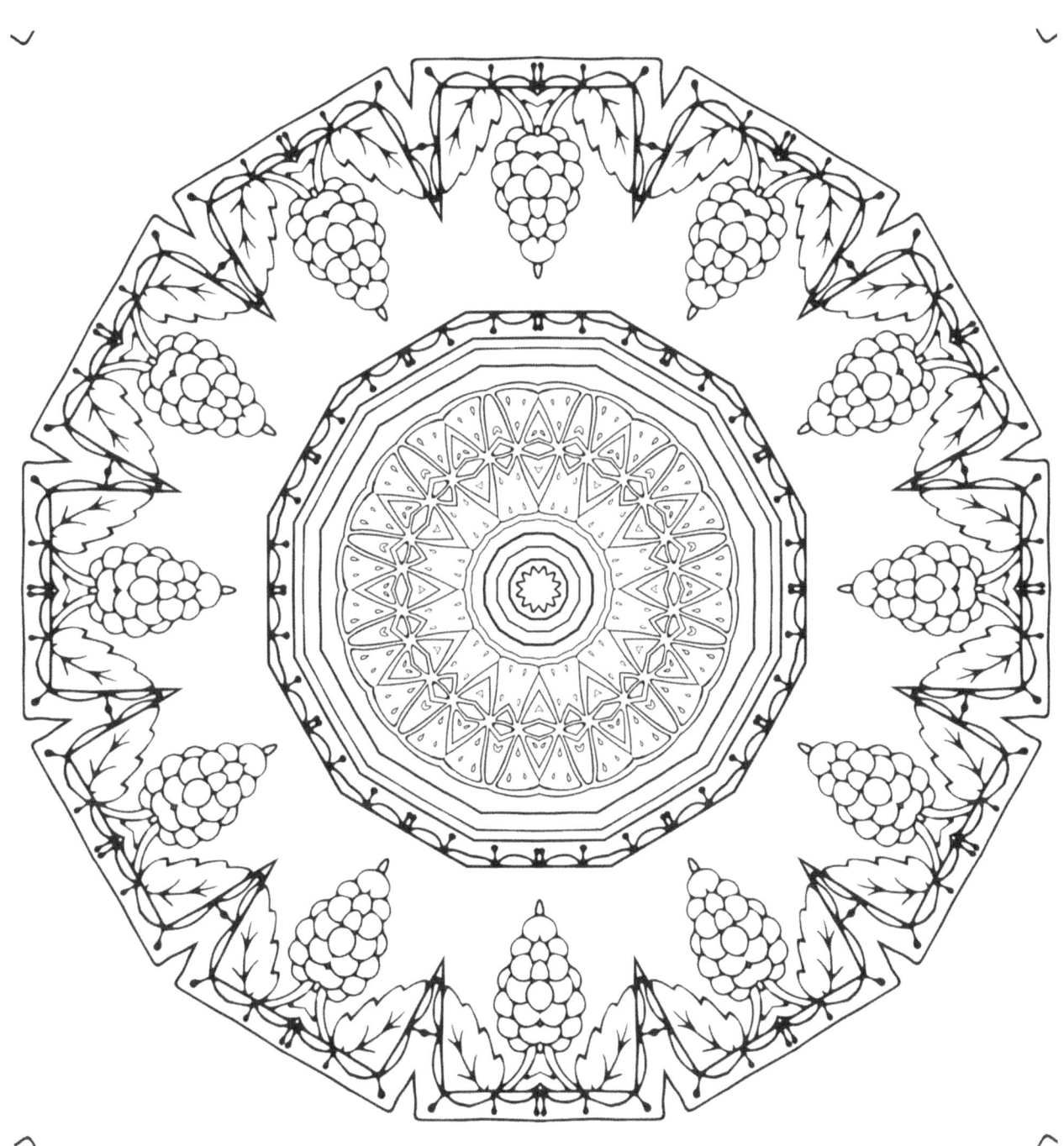

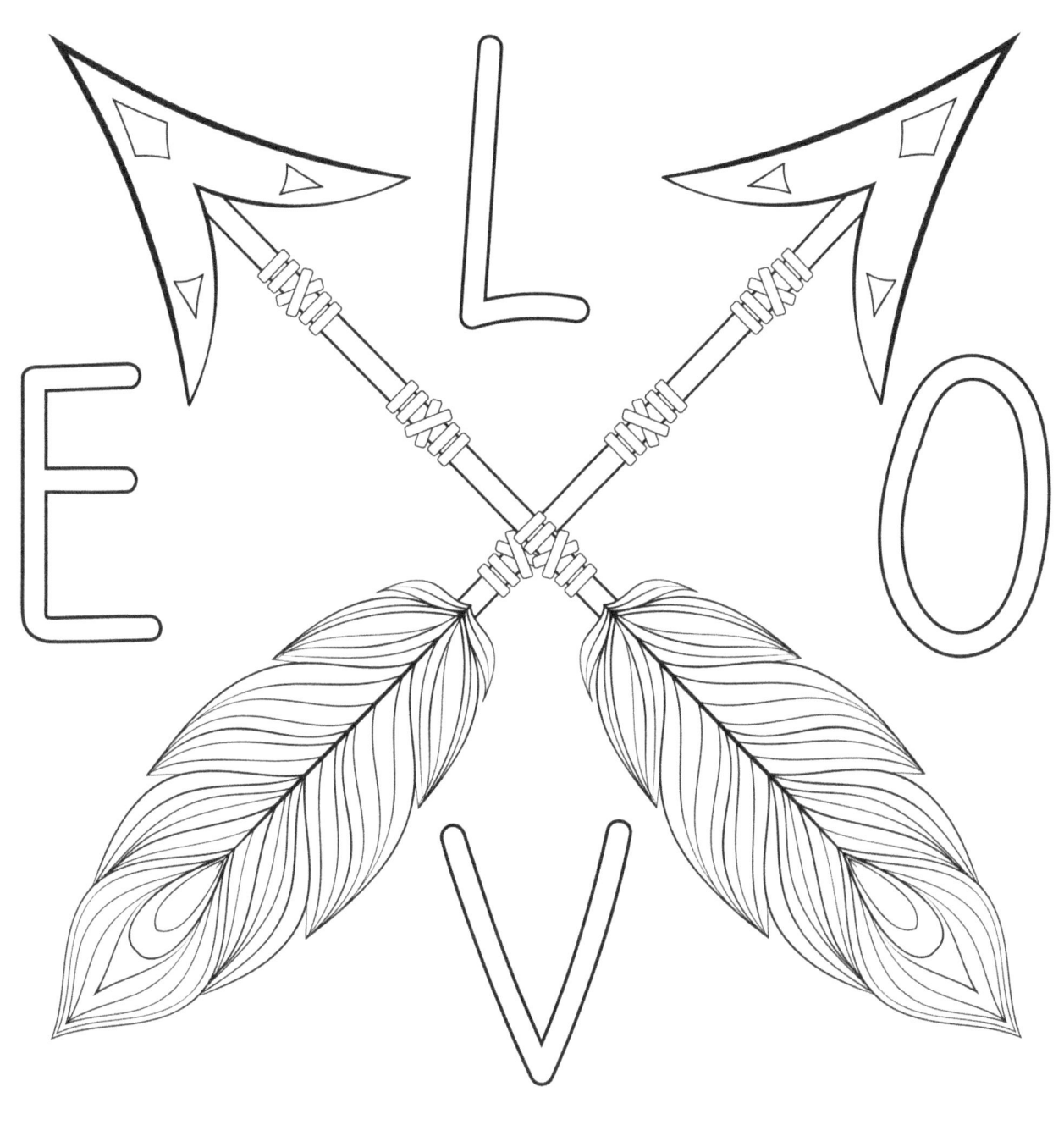

You're such a dick

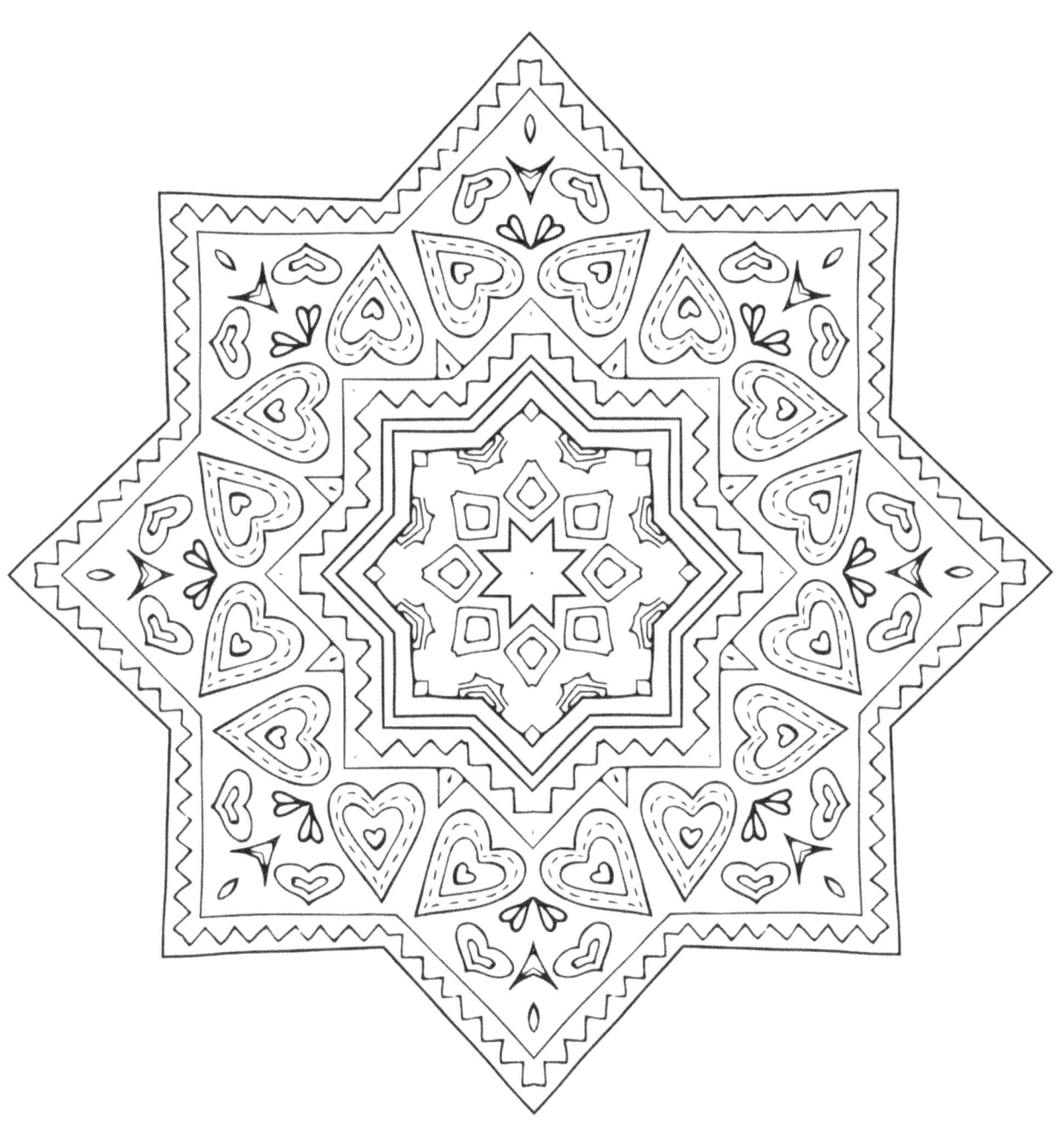

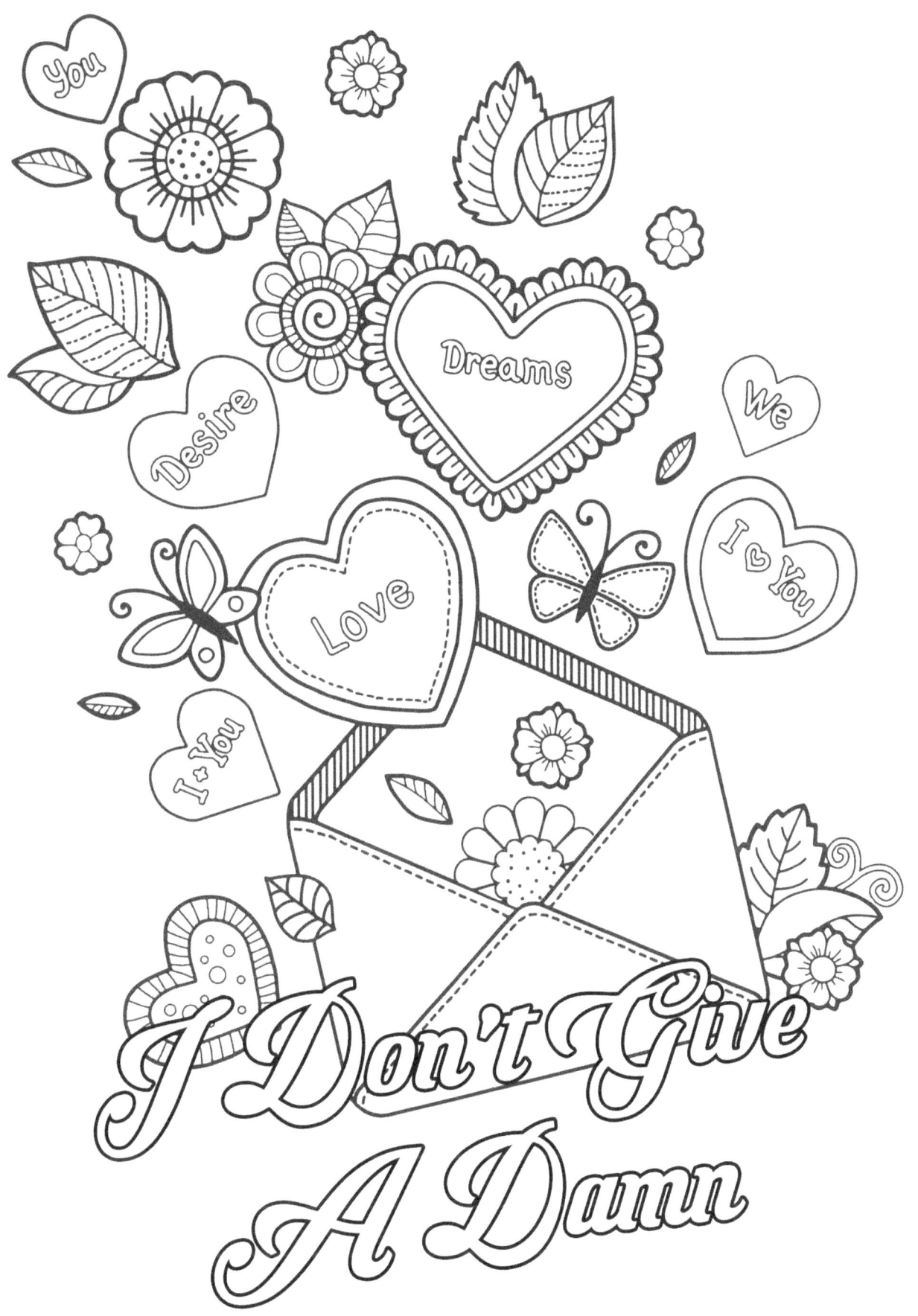

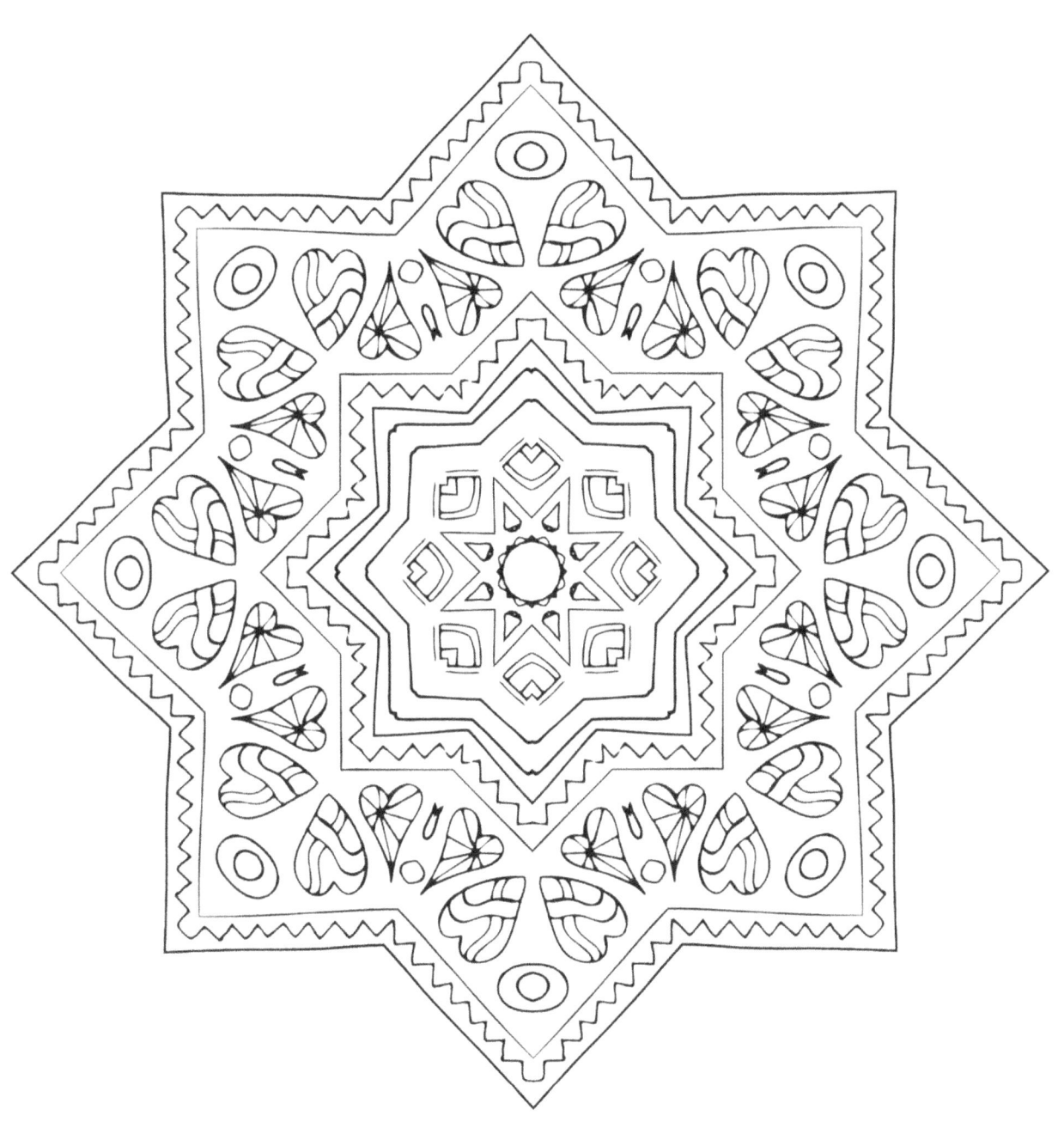

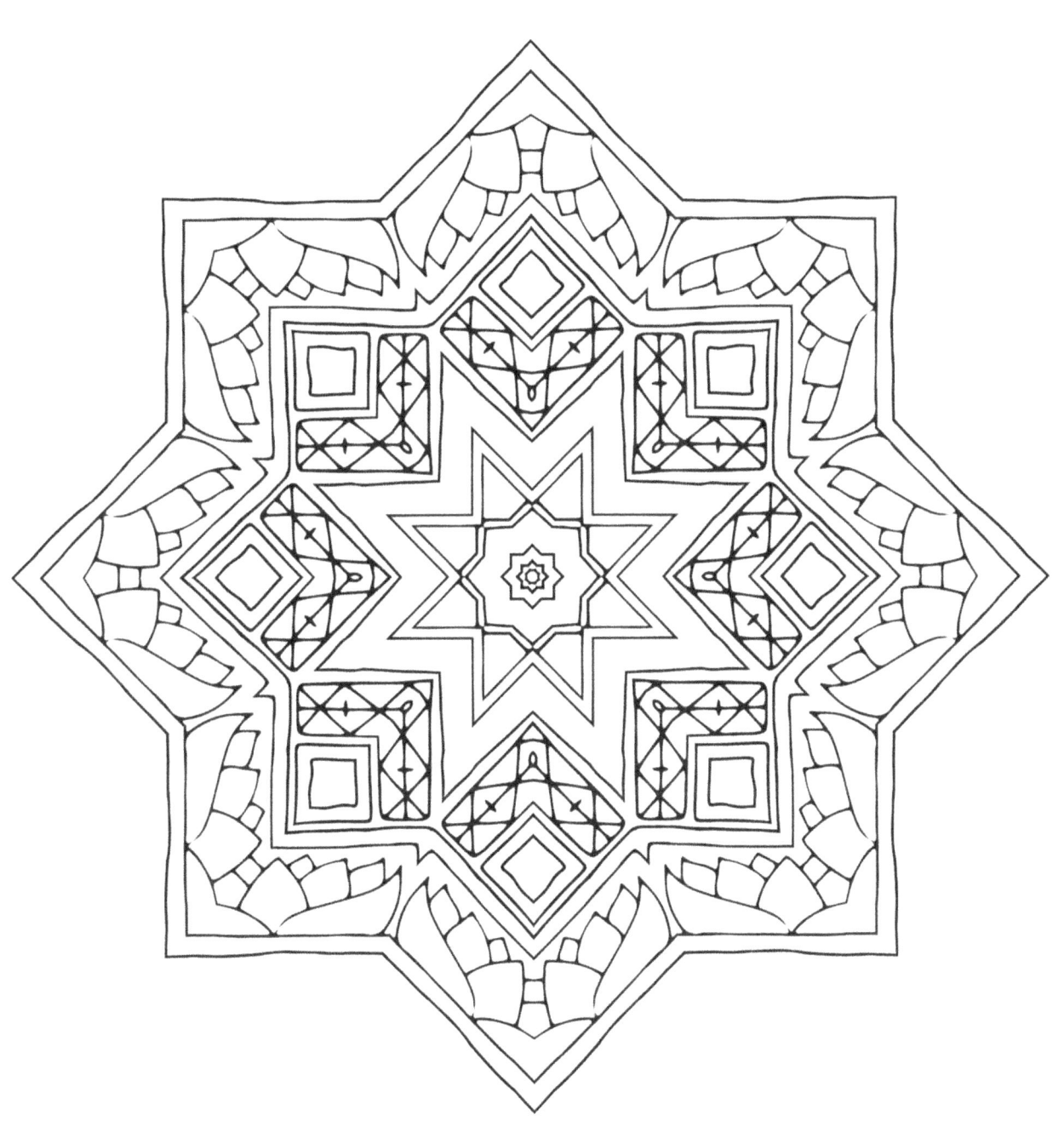

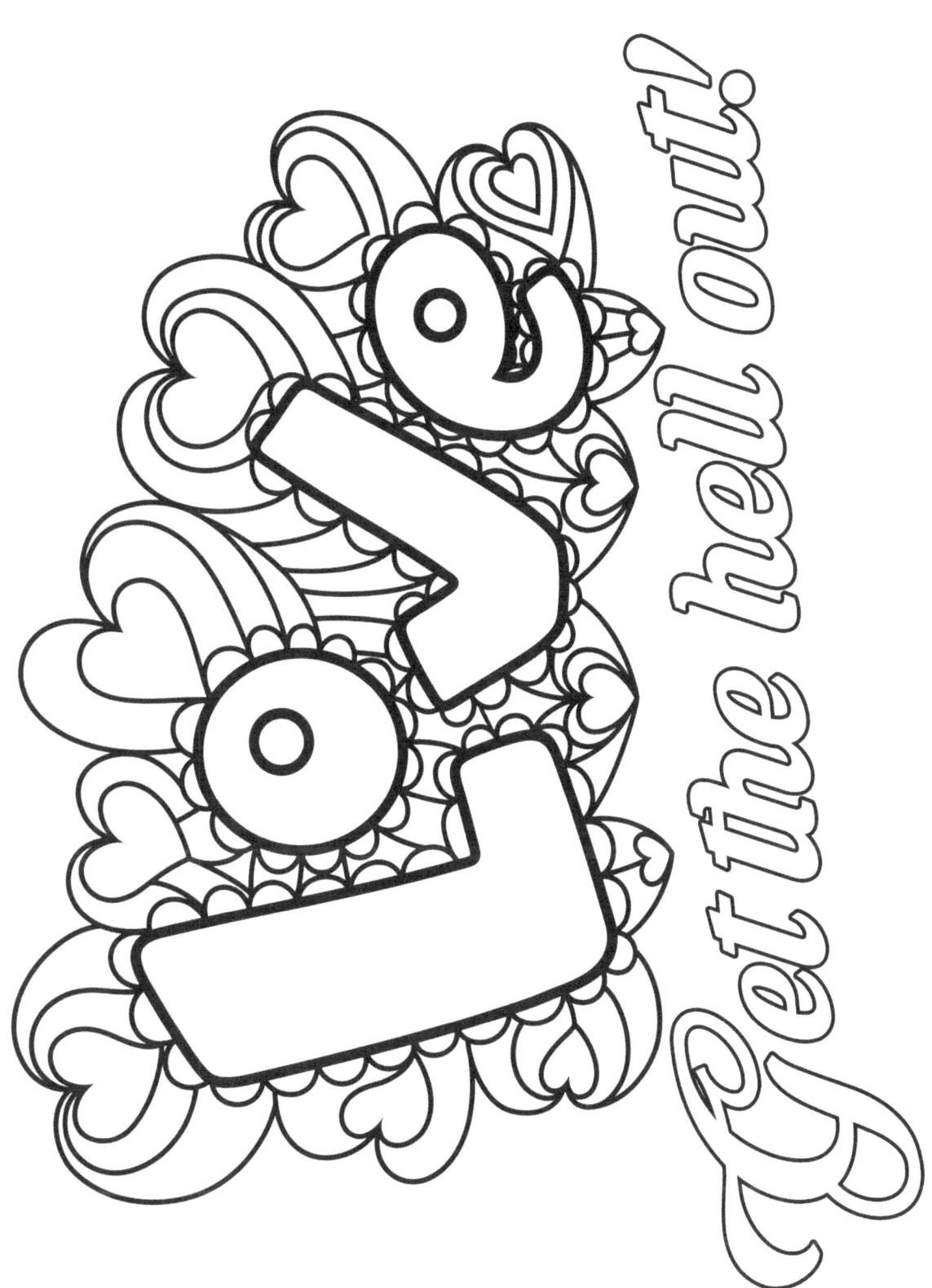

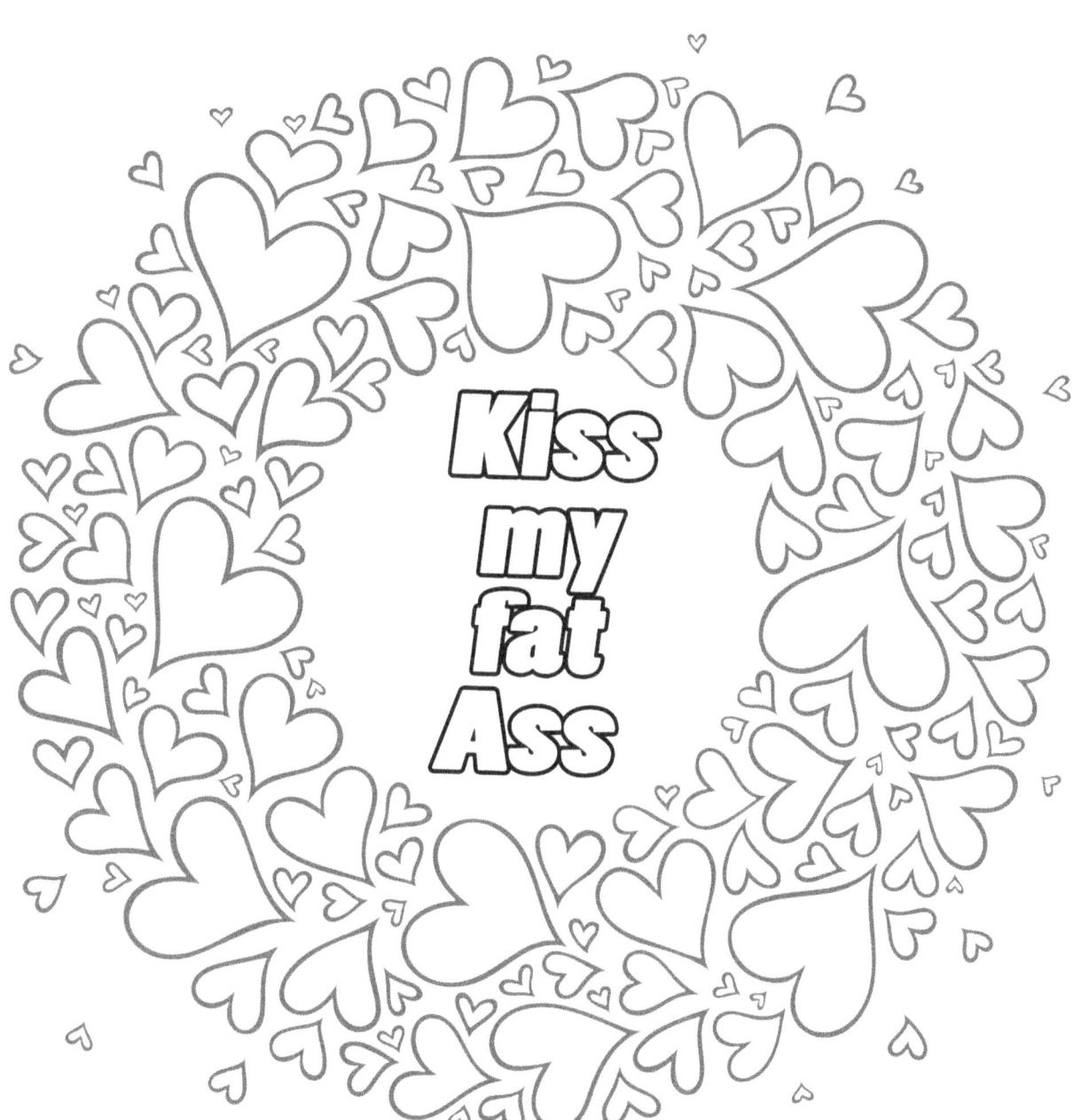

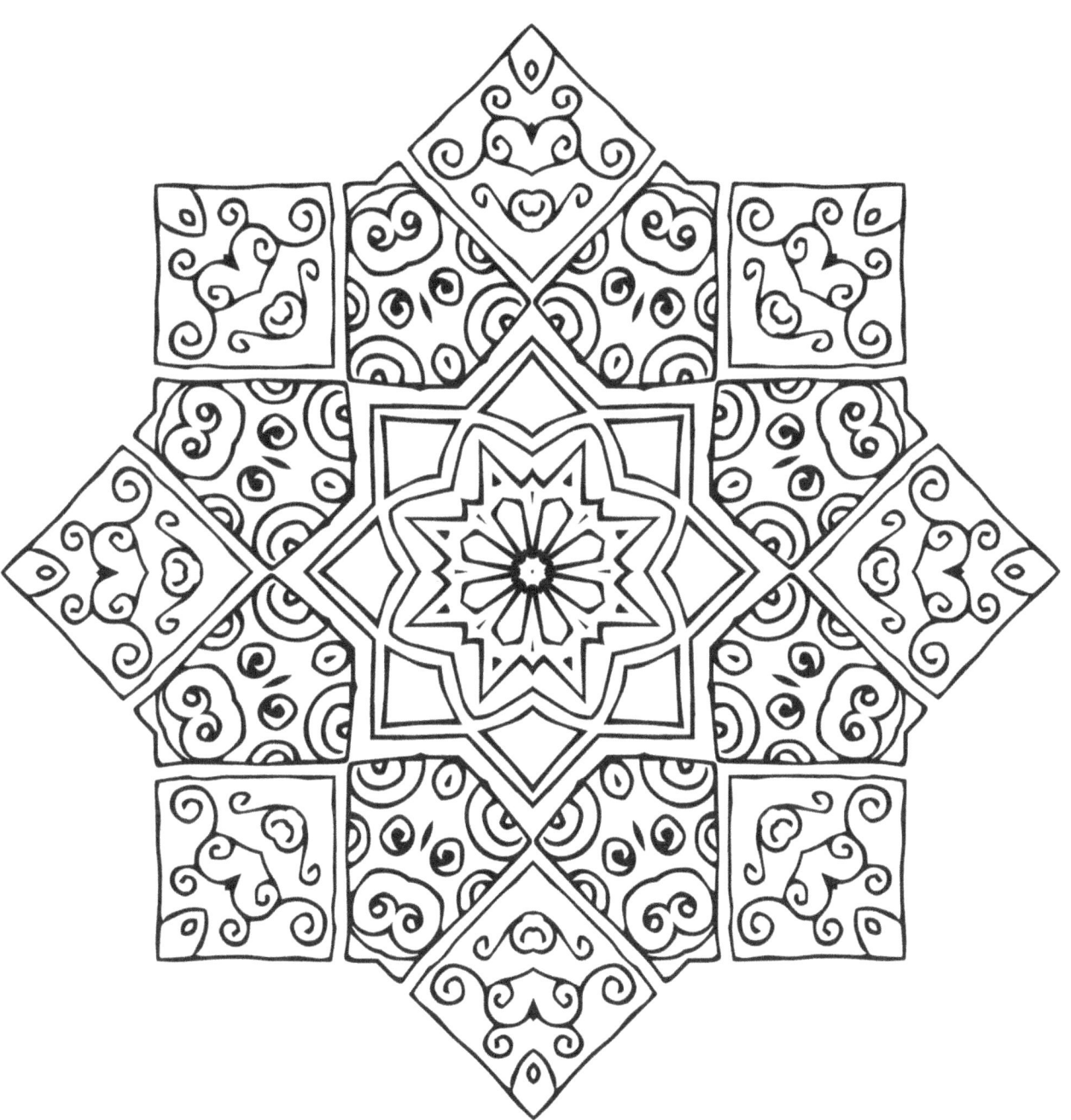

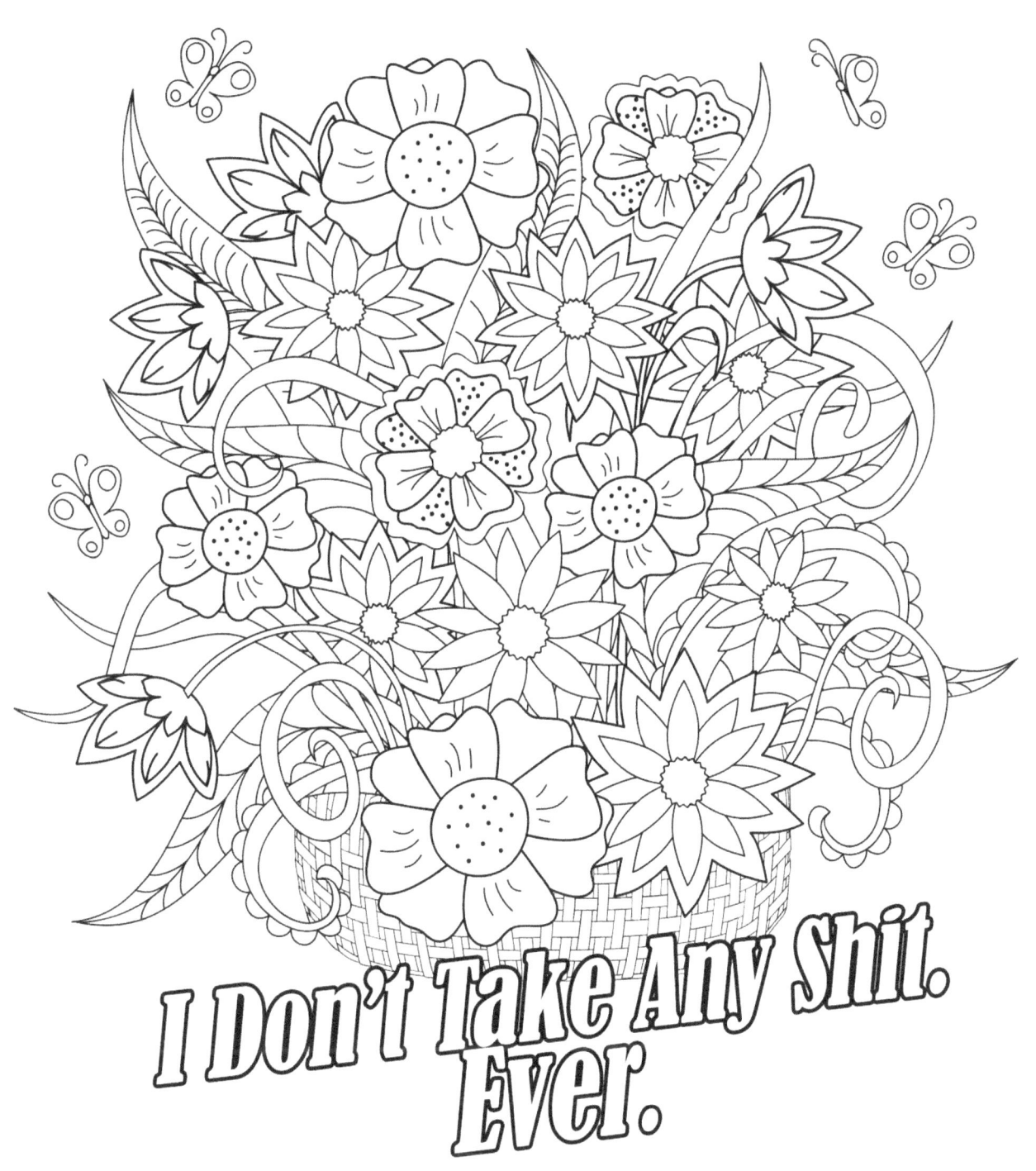

I Don't Take Any Shit.
Ever.

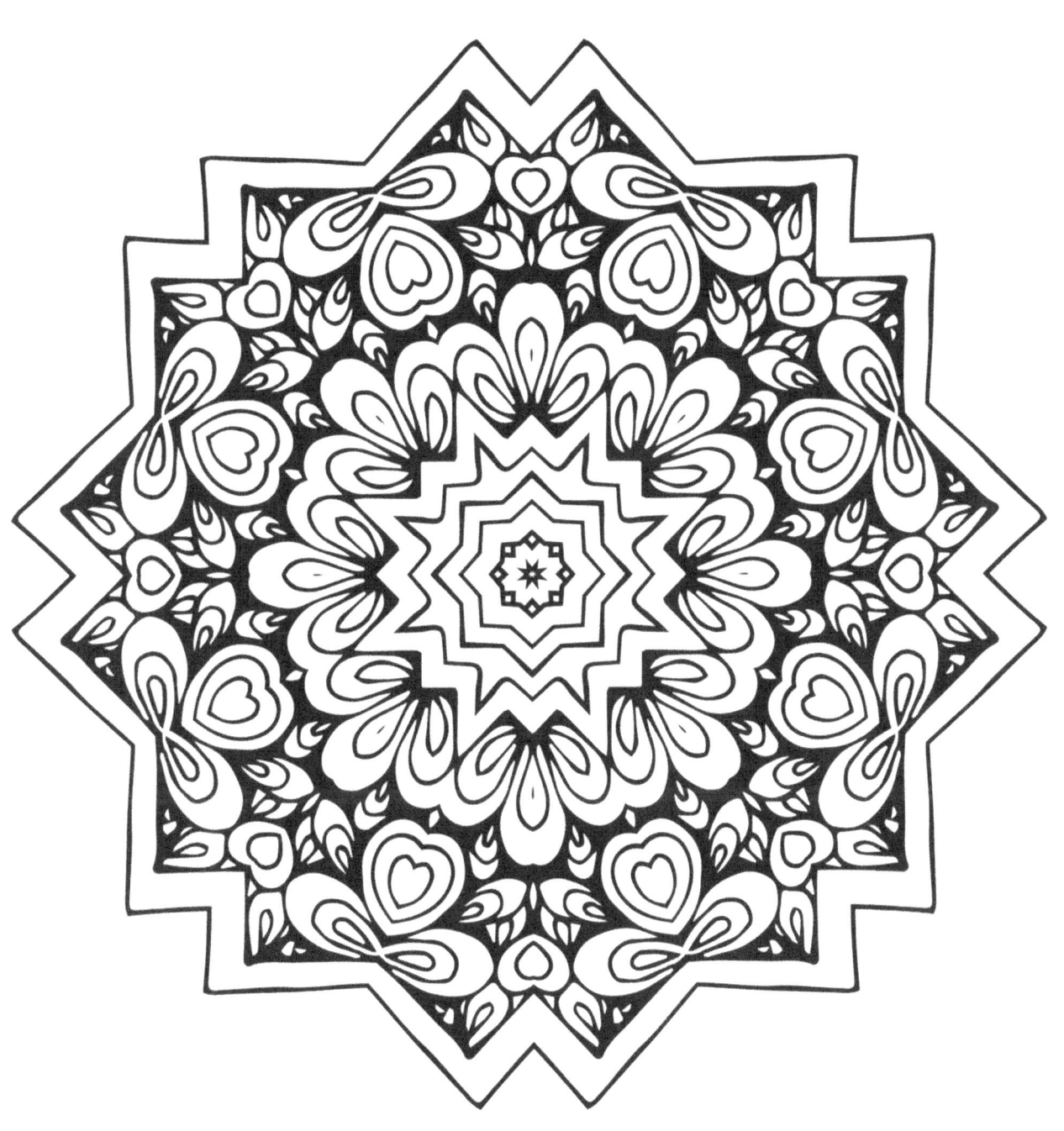

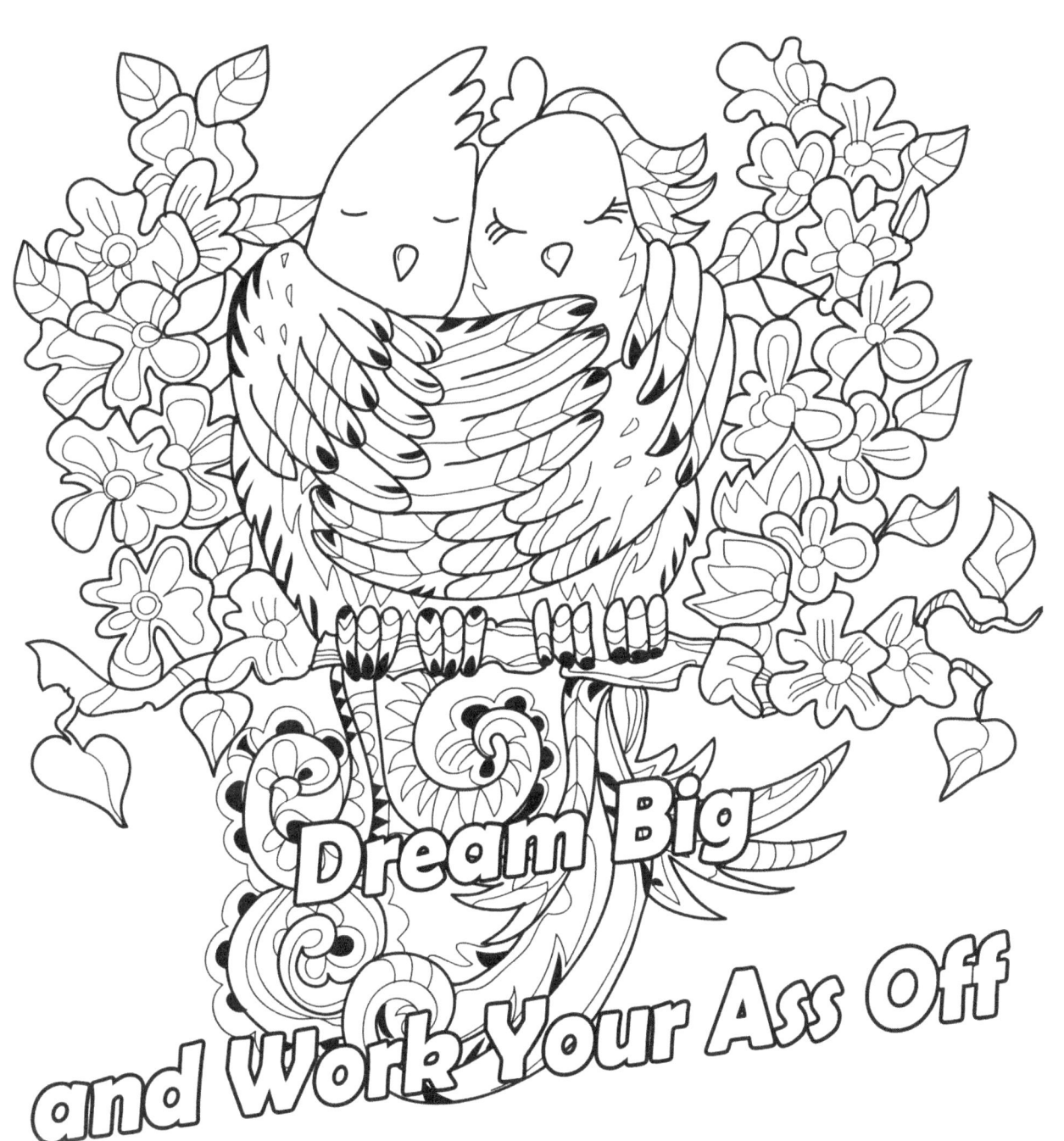

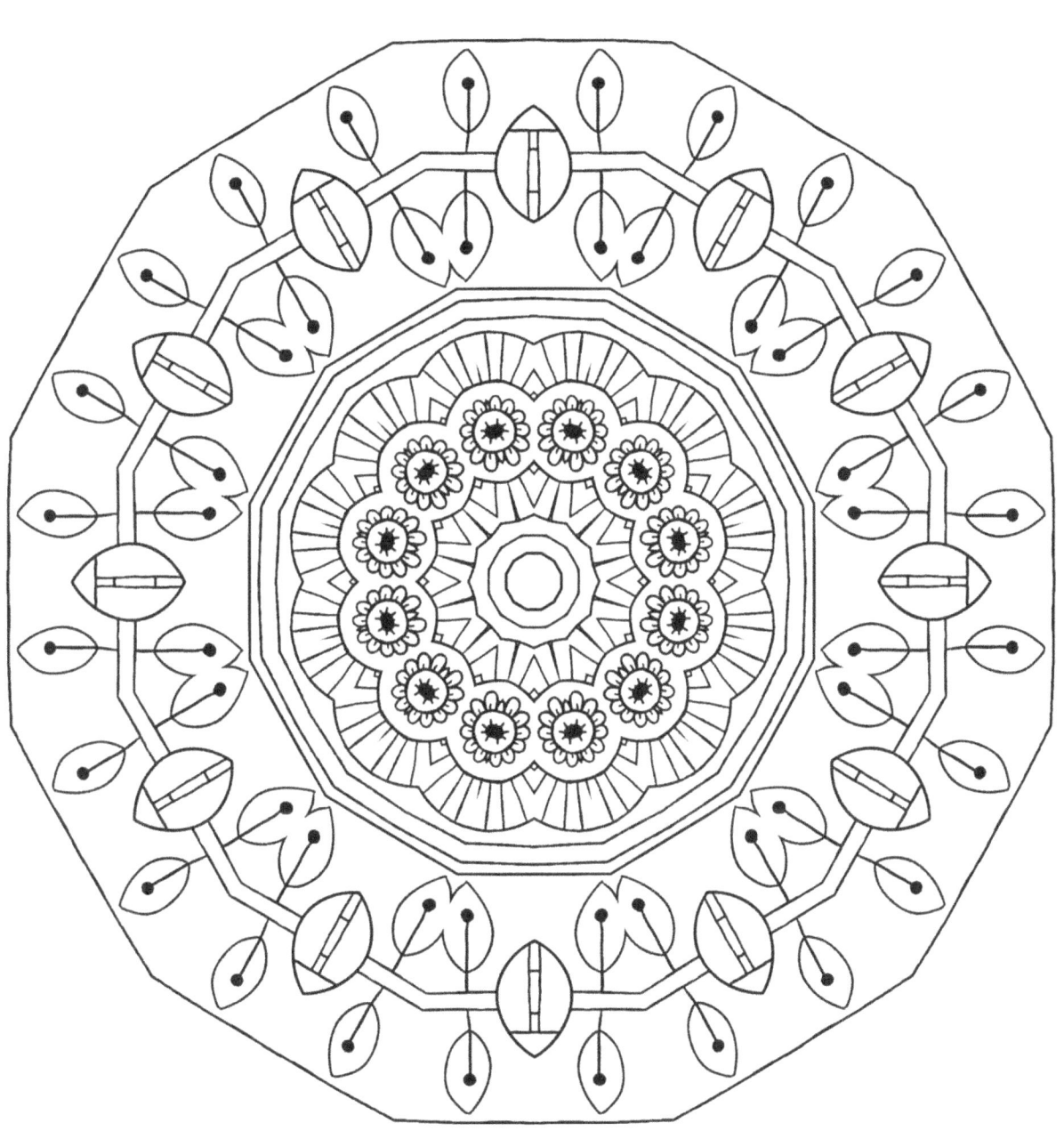

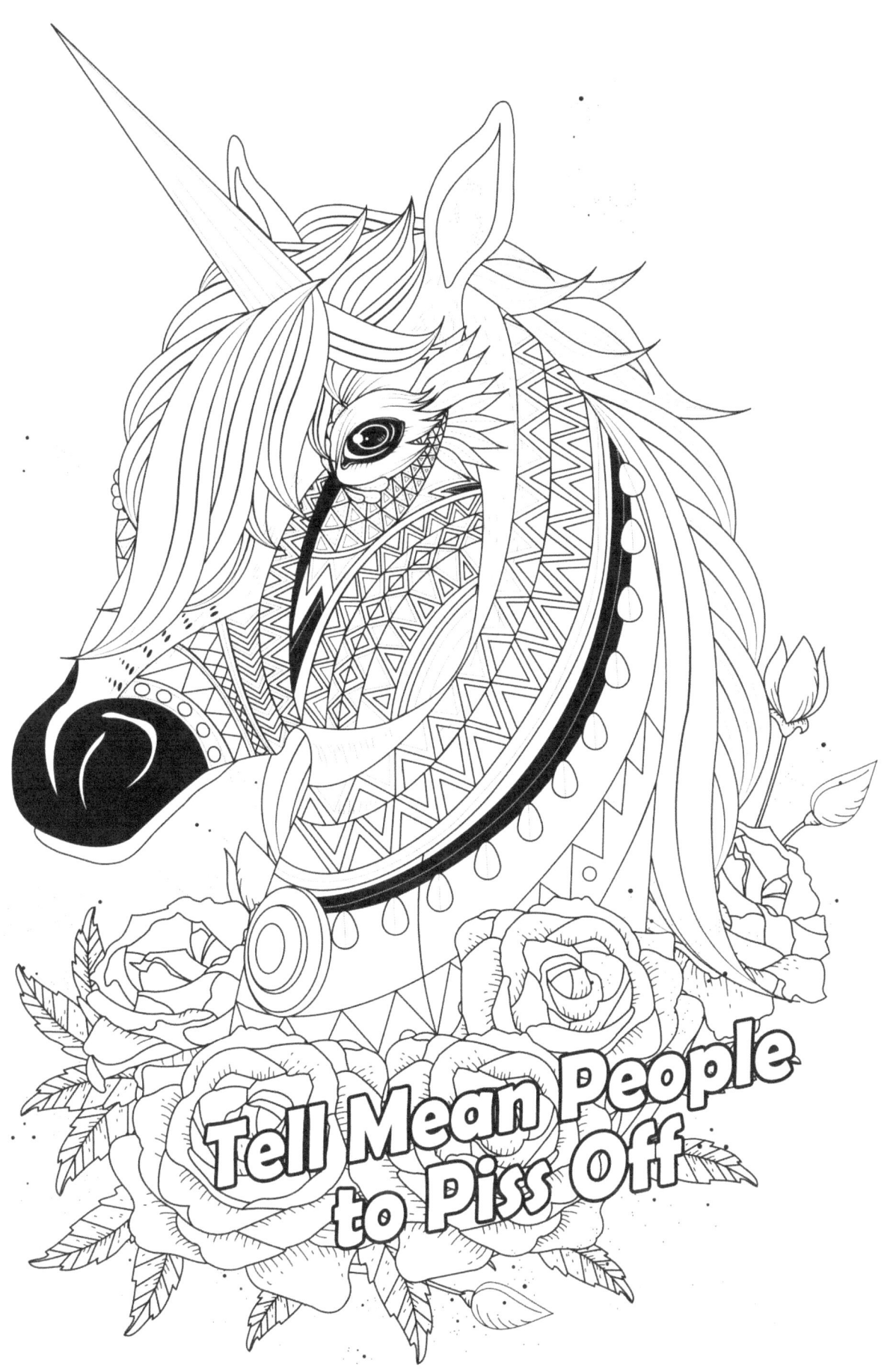

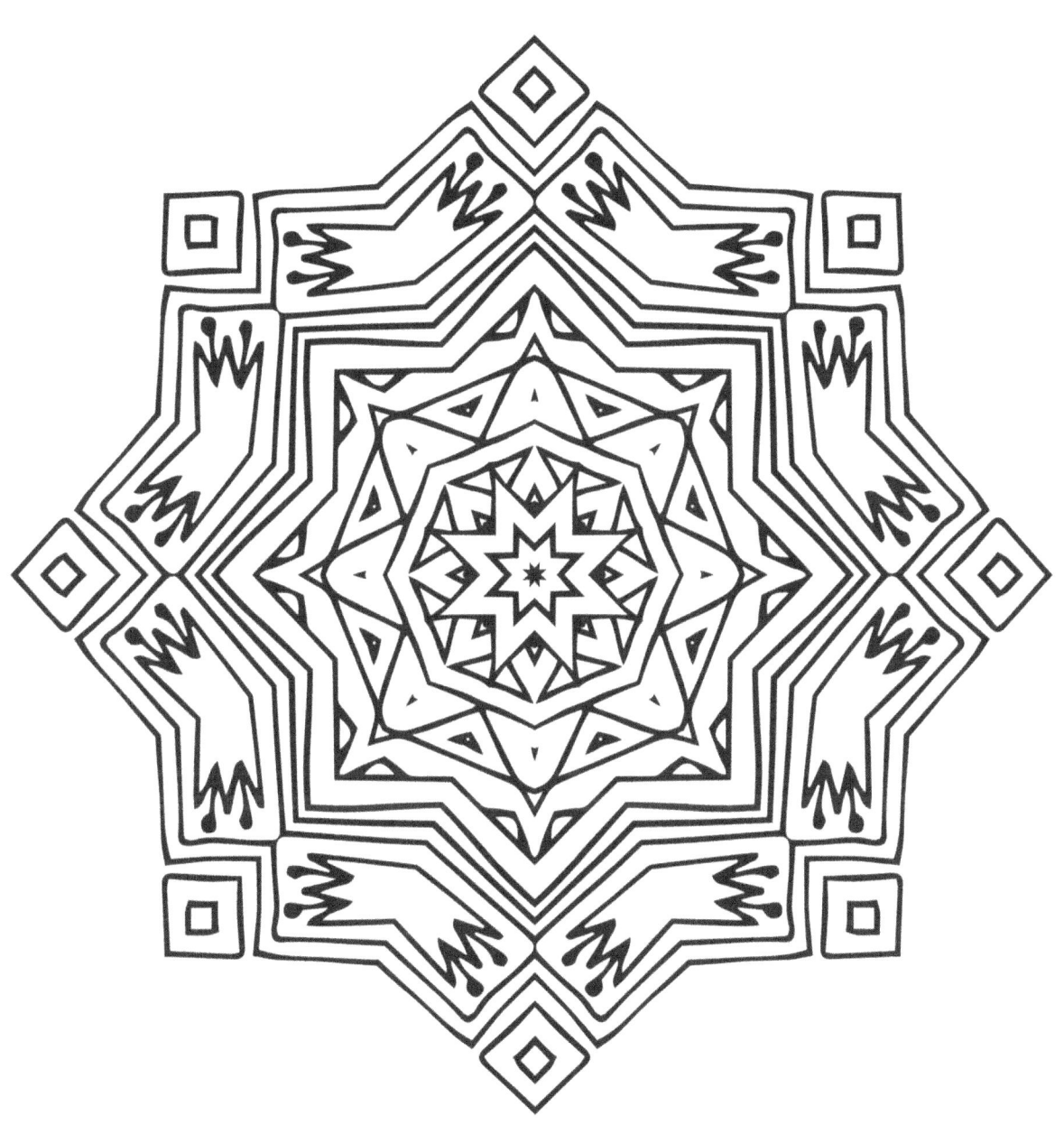

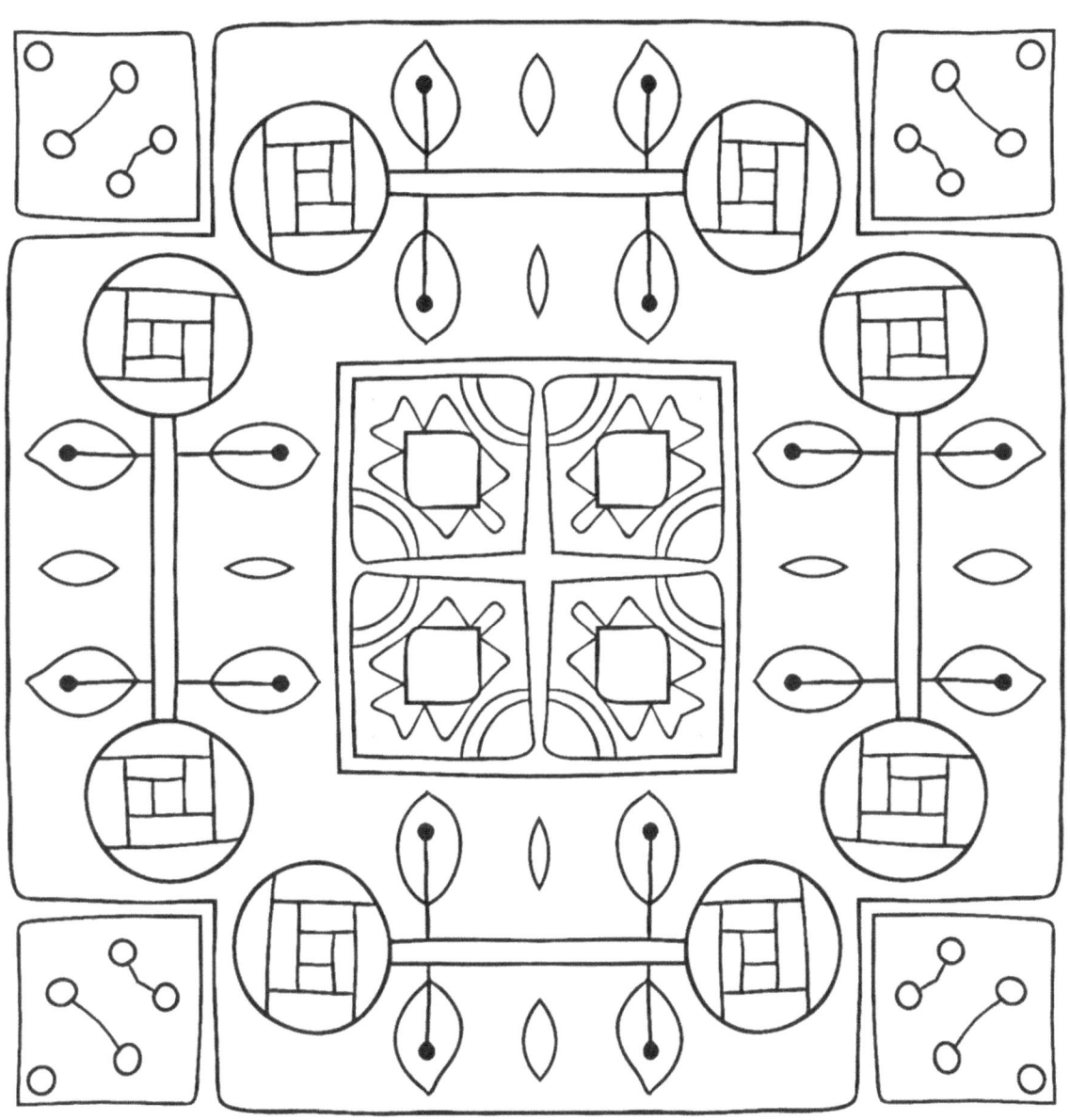

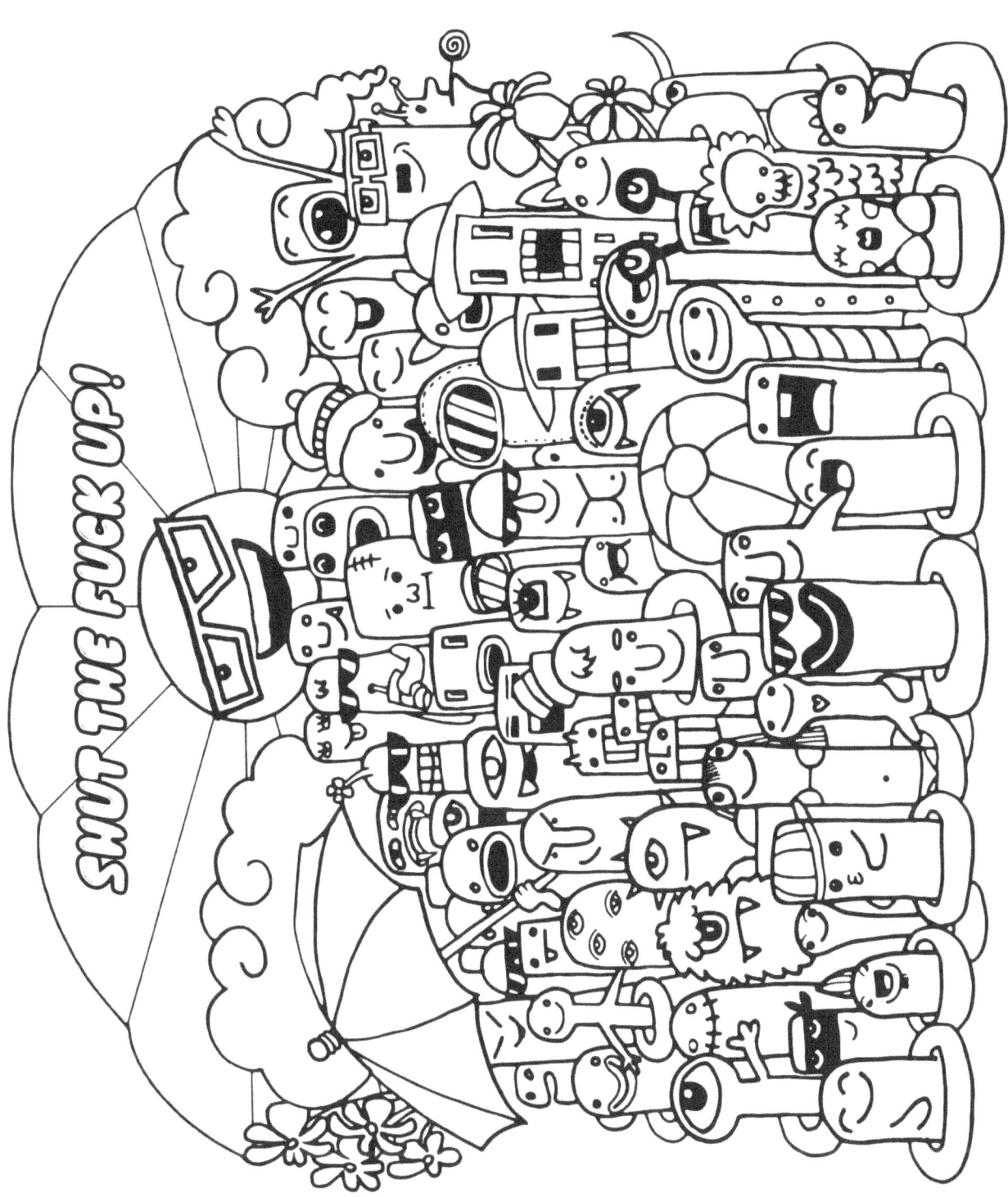

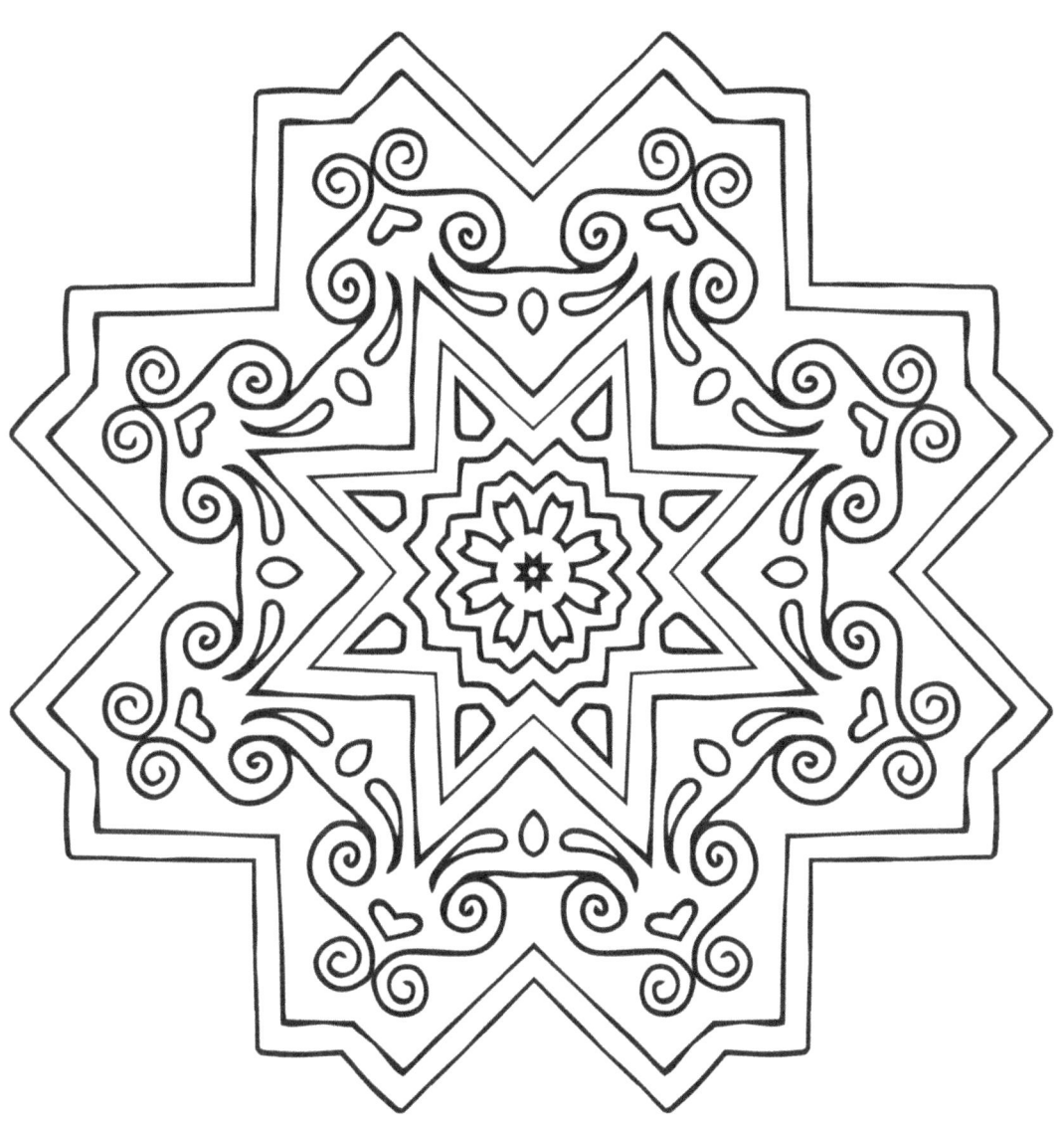

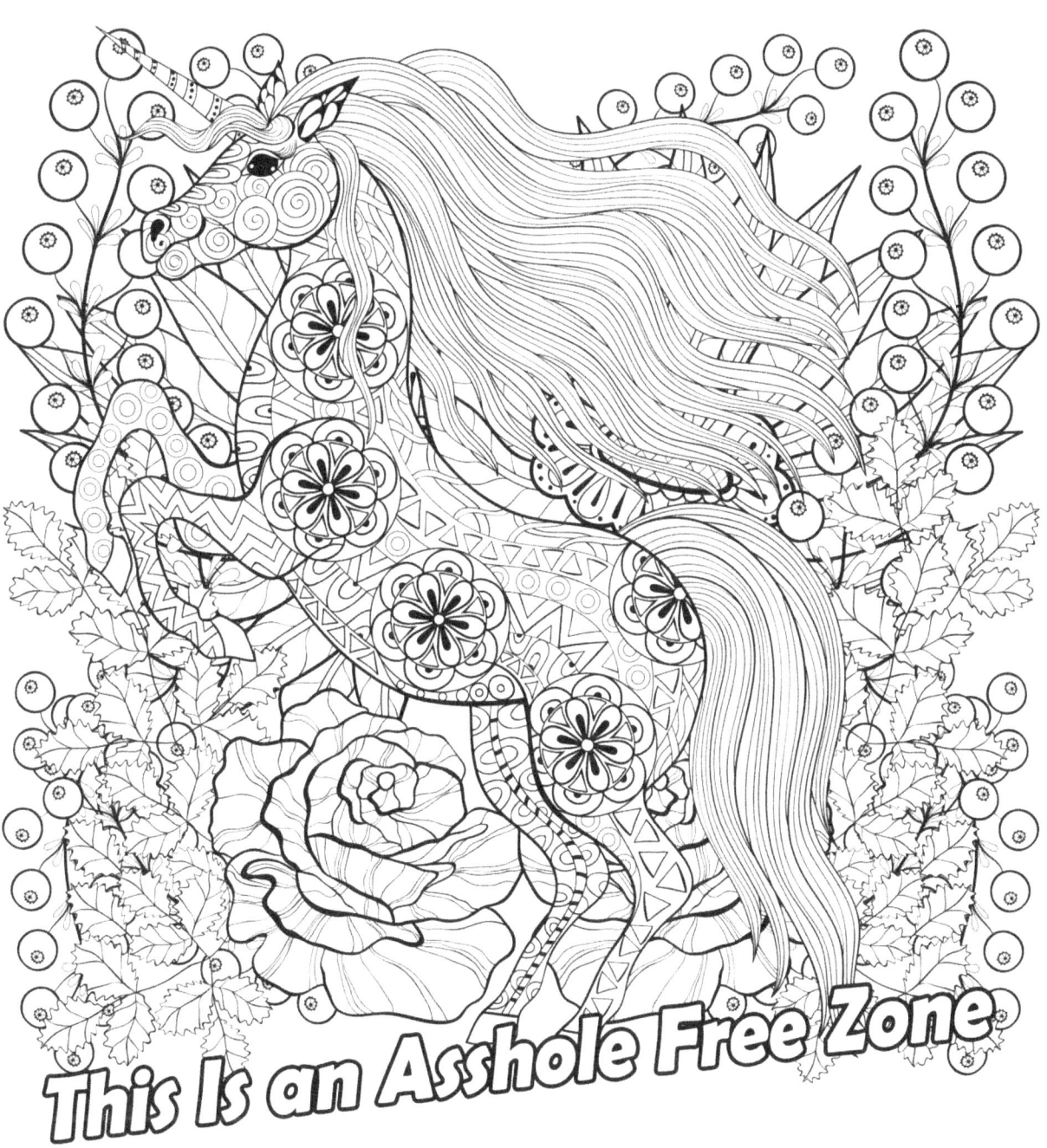

This Is an Asshole Free Zone

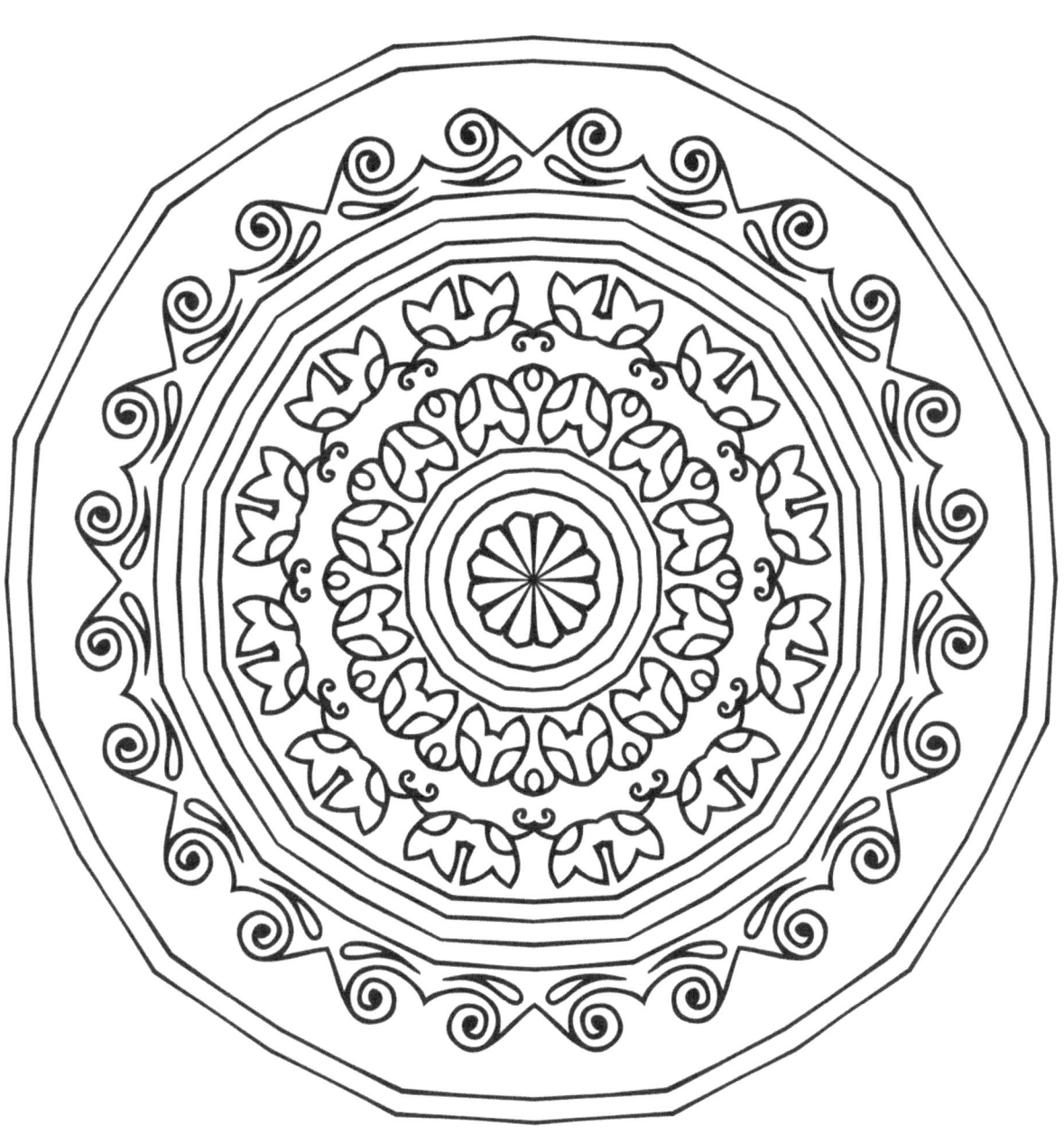